The City as Campus

THE CITY AS CAMPUS

Urbanism and Higher Education in Chicago

Sharon Haar

University of Minnesota Press
Minneapolis
London

The University of Minnesota Press gratefully acknowledges the work of Edward Dimendberg, editorial consultant, on this project.

Unless otherwise credited, photographs and illustrations were created by the author.

Published by the University of Minnesota Press
111 Third Avenue South, Suite 290
Minneapolis, MN 55401-2520
http://www.upress.umn.edu

Library of Congress Cataloging-in-Publication Data

Haar, Sharon.
  The city as campus : urbanism and higher education in Chicago / Sharon Haar.
     p.   cm.
  Includes bibliographical references and index.
  ISBN 978-0-8166-6564-8 (hardcover : alk. paper)
  ISBN 978-0-8166-6565-5 (pbk. : alk. paper)
  1. Community and college—Illinois—Chicago. 2. Universities and colleges—Illinois—Chicago. 3. Architecture and society—Illinois—Chicago. I. Title. II. Title: Urbanism and higher education in Chicago.
  LC238.3.C46H33   2010
  378.1'030977311—dc22

                                                    2010041057

Printed in the United States of America on acid-free paper

The University of Minnesota is an equal-opportunity educator and employer.

18 17 16 15 14 13 12 11   10 9 8 7 6 5 4 3 2 1

To my parents

Contents

Acknowledgments

Through the lengthy gestation of the ideas behind this book and its eventual research and writing, I have been the recipient of a wide array of intellectual, financial, institutional, and emotional support.

The idea of the "city as campus," which underlies much of the thinking of the book, has its origin at Princeton University—a very unlikely place, given the book's topic. There the late Professor Robert Gutman provided encouragement to my early thoughts on pedagogy and urban space, and Professors Robert Maxwell and Robert Geddes gave me my first opportunities to teach. Stephen Kieran was adviser to a thesis that allowed me to think simultaneously about the design of curricula, educational institutions, and the city through a design for a new school of architecture for the New School for Social Research.

Early in my teaching career, I had the opportunity to put pieces of these ideas into action at Parsons School of Design at the New School. I would like to thank Susana Torre, then chair of the Department of Architecture and Environmental Design, for allowing me to participate in the process of formulating a curriculum for a new school of architecture rooted in the urban environment. Among my colleagues there I would particularly like to thank Brian McGrath for a conversation on architecture, cities, and representation that continues today well beyond the contours of Manhattan.

Early research for this project was supported by a grant from the University of Illinois at Chicago (UIC) Campus Research Board. A UIC Great Cities Institute (GCI) scholarship offered a year to frame the book's thesis and also a space for debate on the role of the engaged urban university. I would like to thank David Perry, the former director of the GCI, for his championing of the project and for his thoughtful advice throughout its development, as well as Ann Feldman and Rebecca Campbell, with whom I shared an office, lively conversation, and writing critiques. The Graham Foundation for Advanced Studies in the Fine Arts provided generous support for archival research and image reproduction, for the development of many of the drawings that appear in the book, and for an accompanying Web site on Hull-House and the UIC campus. I would like to thank the late Richard Solomon, former director of the Graham Foundation, for his support of this and related projects on education and urbanism throughout the years.

I owe a great debt to Cecilia Benites, who developed a number of the 3D models that appear in the book and offered thoughtful insights on urban visualization. Joshua Gilbert and Robert Sellars provided capable research assistance early in the project. The book benefited from a diverse group of scholars at UIC, Janet Smith, Rachel Webber, David Stovall, and Michelle Boyd, who participated with me in an interdisciplinary writing group on urban development. I am grateful to Susana Torre, Brian McGrath, Edward Dimendberg, C. Greig Crysler, Robert Bruegmann, Christopher Castiglia, Christopher Reed, and Jane M. Saks, who have been important readers of draft versions of the text over the years and who provided the crucial emotional support to bring it to fruition. Thank you also to Pieter Martin and the staff at the University of Minnesota Press for the care and attention they brought to this project, to the two anonymous readers, and to Paul Venable Turner, who brought important structural insight as the book moved toward completion.

At UIC I thank Fred Beuttler and Jason Waak of the Office of the Historian, as well as the staff of the Special Collections and University Archives of the University Library for providing important research assistance for the chapters on UIC and Hull-House. I also thank Linda Marquardt and Karen Widi of Skidmore, Owings & Merrill for providing access to their archives and for reproduction services. Both the urban activist Florence Scala and the architect Walter Netsch provided access to their personal archives and stories of the development of the UIC campus. I thank them for sharing their passion for Chicago and wish they were alive to see the book completed.

The notion of this book was nurtured in New York, but it was only by moving to Chicago that I was able to formulate it as a thesis. Researching and writing this book has served as a way to learn my new city, and my students at UIC have been important tour guides on this journey.

Abbreviations

CAC	Central Area of Chicago
CHA	Chicago Housing Authority
CIAM	Congrès internationaux d'architecture moderne
CLCC	Chicago Land Clearance Commission
CPD	Chicago Parks District
CUD	Chicago Undergraduate Division (of the University of Illinois)
EFL	Educational Facilities Laboratories, Inc.
FHA	Federal Housing Act
GASP	Generalized Academic Simulation Programs
HHCG	Harrison–Halsted Community Group
HHCPP	Hull-House Citizen's Participation Project
HPKCC	Hyde Park–Kenwood Community Conference
IIT	Illinois Institute of Technology
MIT	Massachusetts Institute of Technology
NDEA	National Defense Education Act
NWSPB	Near West Side Planning Board
NYU	New York University
OIR	Office of Instructional Resources
OMA	Office for Metropolitan Architecture
RERC	Real Estate Research Corporation
SAIC	School of the Art Institute of Chicago
SECC	South East Chicago Commission
SOM	Skidmore, Owings & Merrill
TIF	tax increment financing
UIC	University of Illinois at Chicago
UICC	University of Illinois at Chicago Circle
UIUC	University of Illinois at Urbana–Champaign

Introduction

Lasting institutions like colleges and universities invoke a social rationale for their physical installations, a rationale that speaks to their overarching purposes and helps elucidate the ideas behind their operations. In our culture, we are educated to find in our surroundings the manifestations of character and purpose, particularly when those larger abstractions such as character, purpose, and meaning would tend to escape our immediate grasp.

Kurt W. Forster, "From Catechism to Calisthenics," 1993

In Chicago today the largest campus for higher education contains neither ivy nor lawn. There are no frat houses or sororities, no neo-Gothic dining halls, and no carillon bells chiming the hour. There are no gates to signify entrance into its territory. Indeed, its boundaries are diffuse and ill defined. What has come to be known as "Loop U" is really an agglomeration of institutions of higher education woven in and around the streets and buildings of the southern end of the city's historic business district, the Loop. It is the fastest growing "campus" in the city today, a reflection of college-age students' interest in exciting urban spaces and education directly connected to opportunities to participate in the postindustrial knowledge economy. Though the clientele of American institutions of higher learning may once have been exiled to small towns in cornfields or to hilltop enclaves, today students are flocking to large cities, where urban campuses are growing and prospering, making new commitments to the metropolis and enlarging their domains in neighborhoods once scarred by urban renewal, urban abandonment, or both. And within higher education in general and on urban campuses in particular there is the beginning of a new relationship with the city based on the common mission to acknowledge and accommodate diverse people, ideas, and technologies and to advance knowledge directed toward global interactions.

As a consequence, universities and colleges are occupying spaces in the skyline, in buildings left vacant by businesses that have fled to the suburbs or relocated to new, technologically equipped, twenty-first-century office buildings; they are building new housing and retail developments; and they are finding new ways of partnering with neighboring communities with the aim (not always successful) of avoiding the territorial and intellectual antagonisms that marked earlier town-and-gown conflicts. More than just an object to be studied, the city is now acknowledged to be a unique and beneficial environment for higher education, an extraordinary resource for pedagogy in general and for curricula in particular. Why does the contemporary city serve so well as today's campus? How did the city, once claimed to be anathema to American higher education and pedagogy, come to find itself so intertwined in the future of both?

The institutions explored in *The City as Campus* are offered as a specific case study of Chicago and its universities, but they are also indicative of and situated within larger national trends. They are not merely institutions that happen to be in a city; their founding premises and historical trajectories rest on their relationship to the city and its unique conditions, be they social, cultural, physical, or economic. Thus, the book is not a comprehensive history of higher education or campus design in Chicago but, rather, a story about specific institutions that can trace their origins to moments of intense urban transformation. In these examples the urban campus is imbricated in the city by virtue of the need to produce urban citizens and, equally important, to research social and urban forms that will lead to new ideas about urban migration, calls for urban reform, and ultimately, new models of urban planning and design. What binds these unique examples together is what they teach us about the interrelationship of knowledge and urbanism.

The City as Campus addresses—through a historical account and a reflection on contemporary conditions in Chicago—the physical, that is, specific design implications of campuses in urban environments. It concerns itself with how design, both architectural and urban, is used to represent, negotiate, and influence the relationship between universities and their communities and, ultimately, the success or failure of the exchange between them. In so doing, it also argues that the city itself serves a greater purpose than being the "host" of a university; it also serves as a site of pedagogy and a viable location for the larger purpose of the academic community: the production of knowledge. In the end, *The City as Campus* is concerned with the situation of higher education, with how its missions of service, teaching, and research have transformed over time as it has responded locally to its place in an increasingly urbanized, globalized community.

Although this book is largely a study of twentieth-century universities,

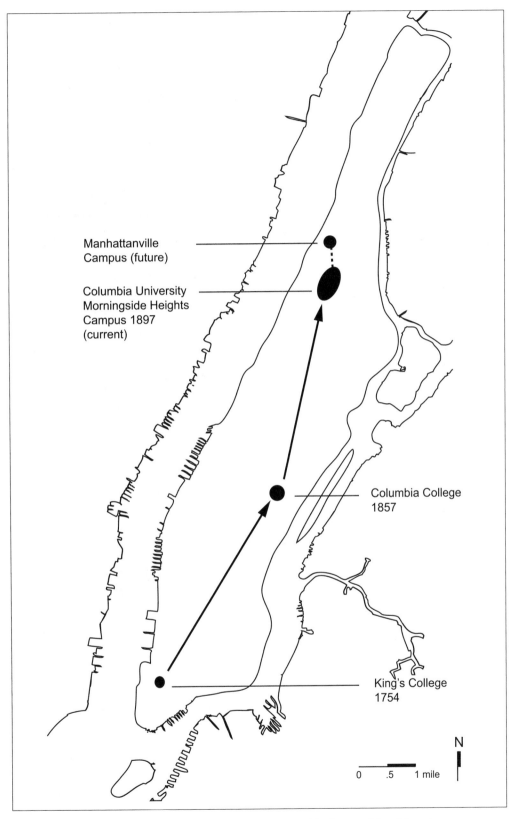

Manhattanville
Campus (future)

Columbia University
Morningside Heights
Campus 1897
(current)

Columbia College
1857

King's College
1754

N

0   .5   1 mile

FIGURE I.1 *Progression of Columbia University up Manhattan Island from its founding as King's College in 1754 to the site for the proposed Manhattanville campus.*

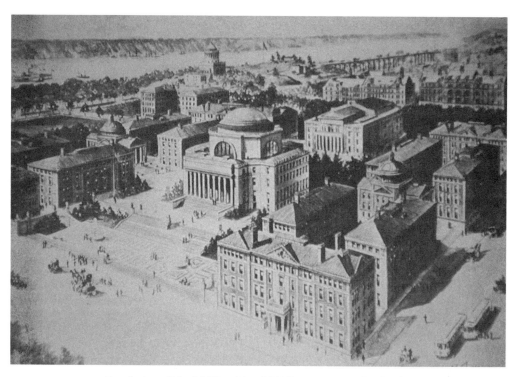

FIGURE I.2 *Rendering of the McKim, Mead & White campus of Columbia University at the end of the nineteenth century. Kings New York Views, 1905.*

universities in the nation were created to directly support the towns (later cities) that founded them, higher education in the United States is not commonly understood as an urban spatial practice. Historically, many campuses were intentionally located to avoid the conflicts and distractions presented by cities, so that when they were situated within cities, they were designed to be separated from their context. As a result, universities within cities are often discussed without consideration for their surrounding urban conditions, which are understood as "other" than the campus. Bender has commented that in this country, "a rural setting is part of the definition of academic excellence," because the idea of the American university sits comfortably within the "Anglo-American tradition of anti-urbanism."[9] These beliefs are forcefully summed up in the use of the Latin term *campus,* or field, to describe the grounds of institutions of higher education; the word was first used in this context to describe one school—the College of New Jersey (1746), now Princeton University—established as an alternative to "urban" schools such as Yale.[10] The "field" at Princeton in the late eighteenth century not begin to settle in the area until the 1830s. Chicago represented the flip side of Jeffersonian democracy's antiurban ideal, for it offered a terrain for settlement that relied on industrial rather than agricultural development. Education played no small part in this process. A post–Civil War intellectual community developed out of a perceived need for domestication that was not anti*urban* but anti-*urban disorder*. The historian Carl Smith described Chicago's status at that juncture as the intersection of "disorder and modernity": "At the heart of it all was the image of the city in extremis, the urban creation of civilization and progress, power and order, that was constantly prey to disruption and disaster."[17]

The growing industrial city was an accepted fact, but it would need to be tamed. Smith noted that this recognition led the city's leaders to strive for an urban consensus that was to spark pragmatic philosophy and progressive reform.[18] Unique educational institutions, like the Hull-House Social Settlement, formed one part of this response, with roots in both European precedents and distinctly American imperatives. The other part was the new modern universities that would take up the cause of educating business and professional leaders, scientists, and researchers for this modern society. For two decades around the turn of the twentieth century, their urban interests would intersect. Hull-House would play an important role in the development of the objective study of the city, which would take root and grow in the sociology and social service departments of the developing research universities such as the University of Chicago.

Throughout the twentieth century, as the nation shifted from an industrial to a postindustrial society, Chicago went through a new period of massive metropolitan growth, inner-city decline, and reconfiguration. In the post–World War II era, Chicago became a center for the large national experiment of urban renewal, and Chicago's universities would become centers for defining and implementing the policies of urban renewal. Again the University of Chicago would play a significant role, but the Illinois Institute of Technology (IIT), with its campus designed by Ludwig Mies van der Rohe, would also test new urban spatial and architectural ideas. Chicago also served as a site for the largest experiment in the development of the "urban grant" university, the University of Illinois at Chicago Circle (UICC, later renamed the University of Illinois at Chicago). And today higher education is expanding at the very center of the city, in a new form of campus entirely intertwined with the fabric of the city and with the project of urban revitalization tied to the knowledge economy. At the beginning of the twenty-first century, Chicago retains its importance as *the* city of the Midwest, the city most able to compete in the global marketplace of products, services, and ideas. In this milieu, the revitalization of Chicago's downtown around themes of culture, tourism, and education represents a new image of the city, one that mirrors changing patterns of urban–university partnerships and projects around the nation, with universities often in positions of leadership. Yet the city remains a contested space. The growth of Chicago's institutions of higher education and of the city is an interactive and at times conflicted process.

Tracing the History of the City as Campus in Chicago

The City as Campus is structured as a narrative that follows the parallel trajectories of Chicago and its universities from their growth in the late nineteenth century through the twentieth century to today, from the industrial to the postindustrial city to the global city. Chapters 1 and 2 establish the origins of the purpose-built *urban* university in the late nineteenth and early twentieth centuries, when the needs of an industrializing and urbanizing nation intersected with the secularization of higher education following models of disciplinary structure and scientific rationalization suggested by the growing German research universities. Chapter 1, "New Institutions for a New Environment," situates Chicago's early campuses within the context of the emerging industrial city. It takes up two campus typologies as they evolved at the Hull-House Social Settlement and the University of Chicago. Hull-House is here understood as a prototype for the urban campus, an outpost in the urban wilderness that acted simultaneously as a residence, community space, urban service center, and research institution, where institution and city commingled. By contrast, the University of Chicago, one of the preeminent research universities to develop in the late nineteenth century, replicated cloistered models of campus design to distinguish itself from the city around it. As different as these institutions would turn out to be, both Hull-House and the University of Chicago are products of the progressive city, of the urban reform movement that culminated in the new civic and governmental structures that became the basis for twentieth-century urban life on the one hand, and for Daniel H. Burnham and Edward H. Bennett's 1909 *Plan of Chicago* on the other. Chapter 2, "City as Laboratory," situates these two institutions within the context of the city, illustrating their importance to the developing fields of urban research directed toward the study of the social and physical conditions of modern life. It looks at how the investigatory methodologies of Hull-House were taken up and codified as a field of scientific study by the social scientists who were building the Chicago school of sociology within the context of the University of Chicago in the first decades of the twentieth century.

Chapter 3, "Modern City, Modern Campus," takes up the next significant moment in American urban transformation, the post–World War II period when urban and national leaders called upon universities to participate in the project of urban renewal and to plan for a huge upsurge in student population that would occur as a result of the GI Bill and then—and more significantly—the baby boom. Projects initiated by existing urban universities such as the University of Chicago and IIT were promoted to stabilize their immediate neighborhoods against further urban decline.

At the same time, the "urban grant university" developed at the intersection of the growth in higher education, the expansion of the University of Illinois land grant, and the repositioning of Chicago as the center of an urban regional network under the aegis of Mayor Richard J. Daley. Chapters 4 and 5 describe the result and form of this intersection, the UICC campus, designed by Walter Netsch at Skidmore, Owings & Merrill, and what it meant to plan and carry out a "model of the urban university."[19] Here the campus is a thesis on how to build these new institutions of higher education within the context of the expanding metropolitan region. Chapter 4, "Classrooms off the Expressway," outlines how the complex realignment of midcentury urban space affected decisions on where to locate the new campus, a story that ends, ironically, with the dismantling of the Hull-House campus as part of the creation of the site for the new university. Chapter 5, " 'Model of the Modern Urban University,' " looks in greater detail at the design of the new campus and at how it combined modern urban planning and the pedagogical imperatives of mass higher education to create a new form of urban campus for postindustrial society.

The massive postwar social and spatial transformations of both the city and its universities would quickly produce a backlash. Chapter 6, "Campus Revolt," elucidates the intersecting phenomena of in-house campus revolts, protests against urban renewal, and reassessments of modern architecture and urbanism. These would have ramifications throughout Chicago's universities, but most drastically at UICC. There, disaffection with the forms of the modern city would lead to the dismantling of the campus core and infrastructure and the attempt to reconceptualize campus space on the model of the cloistered, landscape-driven campus, with mixed results. Chapter 7,

"City as Campus," explores Chicago as a global city—as but one node in a network of cities organized around a knowledge economy—and the way its universities are being repositioned as key elements in this networked environment. In this period of urban revitalization and restructuring, existing Chicago campuses are renegotiating their boundaries and rethinking their physical relationships with their local communities and their unique urban missions and responsibilities to the city as a whole. The chapter also looks at institutions at the heart of the city, at how the campus of "Loop U" is changing an entire urban district while redefining the entire form of the urban university.

We are seeing new dimensions of urban universities' relationships to cities, as the city itself is now promoted as a campus (and cities promote their campuses as tourist attractions). Universities are playing important roles in shaping the larger city outside their walls and are developing new thinking around ideas of urban form and social life. Through the development of buildings for themselves and for their neighborhoods, universities are replacing diminishing local and federal funding, becoming both urban developer and planner. The specifics of the role of universities in urban development and planning will not be explored at length here. However, in the conclusion to the book I will contextualize the Chicago case study within the framework of the explosion of university campuses nationwide and will consider what this says about renewed urban missions, campus–city interdependency, and the prospect for the production of knowledge about emerging urban conditions in a globalizing world.

Throughout *The City as Campus* I am arguing that the urban campus, far from being a subtype of campuses in general, has developed into a unique spatial type, one that integrates the need to produce new environments for the creation of scholarship, research, and expertise on emerging urban space and on social, cultural, and economic practices, on the one hand, and the need to produce new forms for the encounter of pedagogy, research, and the city, on the other. Through the Chicago case study that follows, I will be making a case for a return to the model of campus–community interdependency present in the earliest stages of American collegiate growth, when institutional development was prompted by local community need, while arguing against the cloistered form that many of these campuses eventually took. I will contend that this is the moment to reconceive the campus not as a discrete community set apart from others but as an urbanity capable of engaging both new forms of cities and city living brought about in physical and virtual space.

1

New Institutions for a New Environment: Pedagogical Space in the Progressive City

Provided, That the moneys so invested or loaned shall constitute a perpetual fund . . . to the endowment, support, and maintenance of at least one college where the leading object shall be, without excluding other scientific and classical studies and including military tactics, to teach such branches of learning as are related to agriculture and the mechanic arts, in such manner as the legislatures of the States may respectively prescribe, in order to promote the liberal and practical education of the industrial classes on the several pursuits and professions in life.

Morrill Land Grant Act of 1862

In 1862, Thomas Jefferson's concerns for higher education were extended with the passage of the Morrill Land Grant Act, which allocated a share of revenues from the sale of lands in the public domain to establish agricultural and mechanical institutions. Its significance lay not only in the way it opened higher education to a larger number of the nation's citizens, but also in the way it joined the nation's two greatest resources—its land and its population—during the early stages of the industrial revolution. The mandate of these land-grant universities was to provide research, teaching, and extension services with a focus on "constructive endeavor."[1] This practical focus and the public character of the land-grant institutions distinguished them from colleges and universities established in the pre- and immediately postcolonial period, which were largely limited to serving the nation's elite and focused on traditional subjects.[2] The vast majority of land-grant universities, particularly those established in the Midwest, initially shunned philosophical, political, and theological pursuits in favor of an education devoted to the productive use of natural resources. And these institutions were typically located within the agricultural landscape from which a larger, national economy would be produced (Figure 1.1).[3] As land was sold to finance the education of the nation's "farmers and mechanics," the investment was returned through greater agricultural yields, new industrial techniques, and the creation of new commodities. Knowledge development was directly tied to land development. In this way, the land produced perpetual rewards. Thus, land-grant pedagogy brought together land, industry, and education in productive service at the opening of the industrial revolution. However, by the time the first land-grant universities were under construction in the immediate post–Civil War era, the nation was already undergoing a period of intense industrialization and urbanization. As its cities grew, new urban institutions would develop in concert with the new urban landscape to satisfy the need for knowledge, research, and expertise connected to modern society.

Chicago as Frontier

Chicago owes its existence to location: it lies at the portage where eastward flowing waters meet those running westward; at the joint between the urban East and the rural West; at the center of vast numbers of commodities, including wheat, meat, and lumber; it ultimately became the hub of a complex system of intercontinental railroad transportation. Here, sometime around 1790, Jean Baptiste Point DuSable settled in what is now known as Chicago. By 1837, when Chicago first incorporated as a city, the population was approximately 4,000, and it reached 100,000 by 1869. Between 1880 and 1890 Chicago's population doubled to over one million inhabitants. By 1890 almost 80 percent of its inhabitants were either born abroad or the child of immigrants, a large number of them engaged in industrial occupations.[4]

It was within this milieu that the World's Columbian Exposition of 1893 was organized (Figure 1.2). It would come to be known for the visual pleasures of its idealized White City, constructed for the fair and modeled on European architectural and urban precedents, and for the sensual pleasures of the Midway Plaisance, a celebration of world cultures through a distinctively American lens. Designed by Daniel H. Burnham and Frederick Law Olmsted Sr., the exposition is often cited as symbolizing Chicago's attainment of status as a world city and recognition of its central importance in American commerce and industry just over twenty years after the city's near destruction in the fire of 1871. Florence Kelley, an important early Hull-House resident, would refer to it as "the coming of age of American industry."[5] This celebration of the fourth centennial of the "discovery" of the continent also marked an important juncture in the nation's understanding of itself. For it was here that the American historian Frederick Jackson Turner

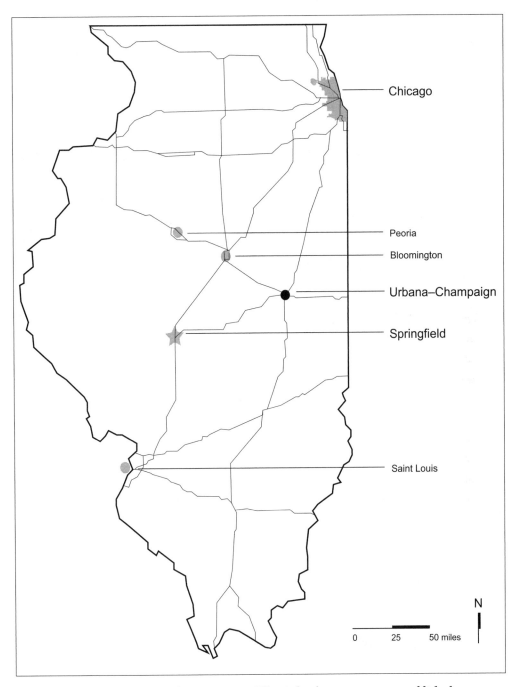

FIGURE 1.1 *Location of the University of Illinois land-grant campus, established at Urbana–Champaign, in the middle of the state of Illinois away from major nineteenth-century cities.*

FIGURE 1.2 *The White City of the World's Columbian Exposition (1893); view of the Court of Honor. Photograph by C. D. Arnold, courtesy of Chicago Public Library, Special Collections and Preservation Division, WCE/CDA III/1.*

delivered his influential paper "The Significance of the Frontier in American History" during the summer of 1893.

Although the accuracy and framing arguments of Turner's most famous work are highly contested, his thesis on the future of the American frontier offers a valuable perspective on American ideas of progress and discovery at the end of the nineteenth century. The work was simultaneously elegy and jeremiad. "Up to our own day American history has been in a large degree the history of the colonization of the Great West. The extent of an area of free land, its continuous recession, and the advance of American settlement westward, explain American development."[6] The settling of this vast, unknown territory mediated by a zone of transition known as "the frontier" was *the* American project, according to Turner. Indeed, the frontier had to this point been identified as the site of the creation of the American identity, due largely "to the changes involved in crossing a continent, in winning a wilderness, and in developing at each area of this progress out of the primitive economic and political conditions of the frontier into the complexity of city life."[7] But, Turner reported, the density and patterns of dispersal of population across the country shown in the census of 1890 now clearly indicated that a "frontier line" no longer existed.

What about the frontier and the wilderness beyond it did Turner feel was so important in the country's development that it made its loss so devastating? "The wilderness masters the colonist," he wrote.[8] The "frontier line" was understood as the zone between the developed (understood as civilized) and the unknown (seen as wild) worlds. The frontier was not just a boundary; it was a space of reciprocity and reproduction. For Turner, the frontier was not just a location; it was a process that took place in a particular space and time. It was attached to an idea of advancing westward, with "the West" conceptualized as progressive compared to "the East." Turner spoke of the frontier as a "safety-valve" and of the development of the West as a release for the congestion of the East. This conception of the frontier both equated American progress with movement westward and mimicked a Jeffersonian distrust of cities.

Turner's legacy is the delineation of a process: the ways in which place and population interact to produce a distinctly American citizen. Crossing the frontier involved going into an "unknown" (relative to whom or to what?) to cultivate and domesticate it; it meant becoming naturalized through the process of remaking nature. The process also suggested an advancing American civilization that would lead to community formation. But as the historian William Cronon has noted, the development of the frontier and urbanization were reciprocal rather than oppositional processes. Migration, whether to rural or urban areas, was a permanent, and not a temporary, settlement process in the United States.[9]

Turner asked his audience to consider the frontier "a fertile field for investigation," thereby opening it to the study and reflection that continues even today.[10] In the late twentieth century, scholars asked us to "recognize [the] 'frontier' as a locus of first cultural contact, circumscribed by a particular physical terrain in the process of change *because of* the forms that contact takes."[11] The frontier defined as a site of "first encounter" is a useful concept for enlarging the traditions that can be considered within this stream of national analysis. This framework helps us understand historical and contemporary urban encounters and their spatializations in the developing American city. But even before recent reassessments of American exceptionalism, in the nineteenth century, chroniclers of the American city pronounced that the city itself was a "frontier" *because* it was a space of encounter between "civilization" and "wilderness." According to many nineteenth-century narratives, cities were wildernesses because of the in-migration of unknowns—both American farmers and European peasants—who were understood as both invading aliens and uncultured natives. They too were sites in need of civilization and cultivation.

As the basis of the national economy transformed from subsistence agriculture to cash crops and industry, population shifted to cities in the latter half of the nineteenth century; a national consciousness of what it meant to be "American" would shift with them. The developing industrial city was an unknown space without historical precedent; its inhabitants were discovering, developing, and defining new ideas, experiences, and environments. Like the literal frontier, the city became a site of Americanization, a place where what it meant to be American was defined and learned. There, the new immigrants were "Americanized" through both their incorporation into the system of capitalist industrialism and citizenship and the public education of their children. The relationship of subject to object, colonist to land, was productive and pedagogical. In the rural frontier, as (im)migrants cultivated and civilized the wilderness, they also "became" Americans in the process. This becoming was also taking place in the urban frontier, as the first two decades of work and research at Hull-House and later at the University of Chicago demonstrated. The late-nineteenth-century Italian immigrants' experience of industrial Chicago was hardly akin to the seventeenth-century Puritans' experience of the New England wilderness, but there is no doubt that the assimilation of the Italians contributed as much as that of the Puritans to the definition of what it meant to become "American." Benedict Anderson wrote that "the son of an Italian immigrant to New York will find ancestors in the Pilgrim Fathers. If nationalness has about it an aura of fatality, it is nonetheless a fatality embedded in *history*."[12]

In his important work *Urban Disorder and the Shape of Belief,* the historian of Chicago Carl Smith described the extent to which important late-nineteenth-century events—the Chicago Fire, the Haymarket Riot, and the Pullman Strike—came into the nation's imaginative construction of urban disorder through narrative forms.[13] But there were also real physical concerns and a changing understanding of the relationship of the family and individual to the land as cities became denser. Life in the early industrial city was hybrid, with agricultural elements mixed within the urban fabric. As Thomas Lee Philpott noted, the contents of a 160-acre farm, for example, might be found within a city lot of 2,500 square feet: "Out on the prairies a homestead like the O'Leary's posed no threat to health and safety. In an urban setting, squeezed between two properties the same size, with the same sanitary facilities available to rural cabins—i.e. none—it was dangerous."[14] Thus, whether the O'Leary cow really started the Great Chicago Fire of 1871—and all evidence seems to indicate it did not—was not directly the point. The O'Leary "homestead" came to signify the real and imagined disorder of the hybridized landscape. This "embattled cultural context" was "contested ground," the embodiment of "instability, growth, and change" and the new "center of political, economic, and social power in America."[15]

This notion of the city as a frontier is essential to the development of progressive pedagogy, which, unlike rural pedagogy, responded to conditions specific to nineteenth-century cities, in particular the new and unknown place that was the industrial city. This new city and its new inhabitants would be brought under control—domesticated—through new forms of public education. It would also be important to the development of the urban research university, in contrast to the land-grant university of the late nineteenth century, as new disciplines and professions matured in response to the effects of industrialization and urbanization to form a new national culture. Together these new professionals and academics devoted to the city would develop new methods to analyze and dissect it, ultimately changing its built form and social constructs. The Hull-House Social Settlement would play a large role in the taming of this frontier and in suggesting one form of urban spatial encounter that distinctly contrasted with the formulation of the University of Chicago six miles to its south.

Settling Hull-House

The two buildings sitting at 800 South Halsted Street—the entrance to the campus of the University of Illinois at Chicago (UIC)—are physical reminders of the Hull-House Social Settlement founded by Jane Addams and Ellen Gates Starr in 1889 (Figure 1.3). Viewed against the concrete background of the university's student center, these heavily remodeled and restored buildings play into today's nostalgia for the nineteenth-century city. They are remnants of the blurry past of one of the nation's most documented urban industrial districts, a site of domesticity and domestication, of an imagined natural order and naturalization, and of colonizers and the colonized. The clearest pictures of cities such as Chicago at the end of the nineteenth century illustrate this life's most poignant attribute: transience.

FIGURE 1.3 *Jane Addams Memorial Hull-House Museum today in front of the east entrance to the University of Illinois at Chicago. The building was restored in the 1960s to what was believed at the time to be its late-nineteenth-century form. Courtesy of Jane Addams Memorial Collection (JAMC-0000-0145-2684), Special Collections, University of Illinois at Chicago Library.*

Originally owned by Charles J. Hull, the house was built on the outskirts of the city in 1856 (Figure 1.4), at the center of a large agricultural landholding. Hull had hoped that the area would develop into a wealthy residential neighborhood, but its proximity to downtown Chicago, the South Branch of the Chicago River, and the railroad lines entering from the south and west made it more appropriate for industrial uses, prompting the building of tenements for industrial workers instead. Hull came to see the house as an inappropriate home for his family, and he moved them to the center of Chicago in 1868. In his memoir of 1881, *Reflections from a Busy Life,* he wrote of his decision to give up the house as a dream of "a great forest home" as the industrial city overtook his semirural enclave.[16] Ultimately, he willed the property to his cousin Helen Culver, who over almost two decades, beginning in 1889, turned much of it over to what was to become the Hull-House Social Settlement, a clearing in the figurative wilderness of one of the most rapidly expanding industrial cities in the United States.[17]

Addams met the young architect Allen B. Pond while she was speaking around Chicago to garner financial and personnel support for her settlement house plan. It was Pond who first introduced Addams and Starr to Charles Hull's former house in the Near West Side of Chicago during one of their several journeys to find an appropriate neighborhood for their enterprise. He wrote about the house:

> [When first built] the house stood proudly alone, flanked by the almost unbroken prairie. In the fall of 1889, when Jane Addams and Ellen Gates Starr quietly established their home in the second story of the house, dingy, forlorn and prematurely old, the first story was used as the office of a furniture factory . . . and the second story had long been the home of shifting and shiftless tenants. The meadows and prairies had been swallowed up in a wilderness of brick and lumber.[18]

FIGURE 1.4 *Charles Hull's 1856 house on the outskirts of Chicago as it was envisioned in a painting in the late nineteenth century. Courtesy of Jane Addams Memorial Collection (JAMC-0000-0146-1145), Special Collections, University of Illinois at Chicago Library.*

Hull's house perfectly embodied the characteristics of the neighborhood and of its current residents, as Pond saw them: "shifting and shiftless," a constant inward and outward stream of inhabitants. The building was a remnant of a brief pastoral past. All around, the original prairie and swamp-like wilderness had succumbed to industrial overgrowth. The building had two physical qualities that aligned with Addams's idea of what a settlement house should be. As a freestanding house, it satisfied the needs of its anticipated residents for an independent living condition within the city. As a house situated among tenements, it fulfilled the requirement that these residents live among the poor.

The Hull-House Social Settlement was a transformation of an English model of university "extension" into an American context. Toynbee Hall, established in the East End of London in 1884 by Samuel and Henrietta Barnett, served as the model for the American settlement. Toynbee Hall offered an opportunity for university men to live among and work with the poor in the interest of promoting social and class understanding through social clubs, lectures, and other forms of aid. Hull-House was to continue this concept of urban extension, but with two significant differences. Hull-House's neighbors were recent immigrants to the United States who, in addition to contending with life in the industrial city, were adjusting to an alien culture. Further, Hull-House residents were largely women, many of whom had recently graduated from college. In the American context, the settlement house afforded its residents what I have elsewhere referred to as a "home in public."[19] As the college-educated woman moved out into the public, she still required a space from which to do so. After all, it was not long before Addams and Starr established Hull-House that Marshall Field had established a tea room to make it respectable for women to shop in his Chicago department store unaccompanied by men.

If Hull-House was not an outpost of a specific institution of higher education, why is it important to this narrative? First, for many young residents, the settlement served as a transitional space, enabling them to negotiate between their education and a form of public life denied to them because of their gender. As such, it was an extension of their college life. Second, many of the new forms of urban service provided by settlements would become implicit in the academic missions of many colleges and universities. Third, although Hull-House itself was not allied with an educational institution, many settlements for which it was the prototype were. Important among these in Chicago were the settlements organized by the University of Chicago and Northwestern University. As its architects would write, Hull-House set the precedent and served as prototype for the programmatic and spatial organizations of many settlement houses that would follow. As an outpost of institutions of higher education, these sites were by definition not part of a university campus. However, Hull-House and many similar institutions had campuslike traits and had architectural requirements similar to those at small academic institutions. Yet their distinctly public or neighborhood directedness compelled a different physical negotiation with urban space that, although unique in the late nineteenth century, might have a bearing on how we think about campus–city interactions in the early twentieth century. Finally, as we will see in chapter 2, Hull-House itself was instrumental in developing forms of urban analysis and knowledge about the city that would come to fruition in the research university, notably in the Chicago school of urban sociology at the University of Chicago.

Hull-House started as a seemingly modest proposition. Addams and Starr established their new enterprise by settling in Hull's former house. In the view of Myra Jehlen and other scholars, broadly, it was the act of settling, and not of discovery, that made possible the constant reinventions of the concepts "America" and "the American."[20] According to *The Oxford English Dictionary* (*OED*), the *act* of settlement—settling—involves "fixing (a thing, material or immaterial) in a secure or steady position" or being in the *state* "of being so fixed." This definition applied to the settling of early colonists in New England and accompanying acts of regulation that "[put] things on a permanent footing" so as to establish "security or tranquility." The *OED* recognizes two definitions of the *noun* "settlement" that are of particular note here:

> In the outlying districts of America and the (former) colonial territories: A small village or collection of houses. Also, the huts forming the living quarters of the slaves on a plantation.

> An establishment in the poorer quarters of a large city where educated men or women live in daily personal contact with the working classes for co-operation in social reform.[21]

These two definitions establish an equation that illustrates the way in which the settlement house was conceived in the nineteenth-century city as a symbol of order. As residents educated their neighbors, they educated themselves, reproducing the subject and object relationships of the traditional frontier. Settlers were colonists of and colonizers in their own country.

Key to understanding the developing role of Hull-House in Chicago are Jane Addams's own descriptions of Hull-House in her best-known text, *Twenty Years at Hull-House*, published in 1909, which collected many of her writings. Two of the earliest—"The Objective Value of a Social Settlement" and "The Subjective Necessity for Social Settlements"[22]—laid down the social precepts and positions, essentially two axes, on which the settlement was founded. In "The Objective Value of Social Settlement," Addams began with a physical description of the house and stated goals that spoke directly to the urban-industrial conditions she hoped the project would help ameliorate: "The Settlement . . . is an experimental effort to aid in the solution of the social and industrial problems which are engendered by the modern conditions of life in a great city." Although she insisted that these problems were not confined to any one portion of a city, "the site for a settlement was selected . . . because of its diversity, and the variety of activity for which it presented an opportunity . . . to respond to the neighborhood as a whole."[23] To accomplish their goals, settlement workers, or "residents," as they were called, would need to both live and work in the neighborhood with their "neighbors," who were the *objects* of their work. In turn, the residents of the settlement were its *subjects* (Figure 1.5). Residents lived communally at the house and, in carrying out the settlement's projects, had the opportunity to experience urban public life while transforming their own and their neighbors' understanding of democracy within the newly forming industrial context.[24]

Although women had not yet received full suffrage, the position and plight of a young woman of upper-middle-class background in this period was quite different from those of her mother and grandmother. As has been documented, and as Addams personally testified, industrialization altered, even though it did not completely eliminate, the need for women's productive work within the home.[25] Thus "freed," many young women of the post–Civil War era traveled (typically to western Europe) or attended the growing number of women's colleges to further their education. Addams asked, "For what?" Hull-House and other social, collegiate, and religious settlements that opened around the same time provided an opportunity for these women—particularly those who chose not to marry—to migrate to the burgeoning industrial cities of North America. Yet, unlike the possibilities available to working-class women in factory or retail work, the

FIGURE 1.7 *First addition to the Hull-House Social Settlement: Reading Room and Butler Art Gallery. The image illustrates the relationship of the growing settlement to neighboring buildings along Halsted Street. Courtesy of Jane Addams Memorial Collection (JAMC-0000-0129-0529), Special Collections, University of Illinois at Chicago Library.*

allowed its residents to experiment with a diverse array of domestic and institutional urban programming and its architects to explore the physical design and stylistic articulation of spaces to house these activities.

After 1893, the settlement's extensive building program brought many previously dispersed activities under its roofs. Thus, Allen Pond would write in 1902 that Hull-House was the model for, even if not the ideal, settlement architecture. For all practical purposes, it established the diverse programming that would become the hallmark of the over one hundred settlements established in the late nineteenth and early twentieth centuries. It was also remarkable for its fluidity in relationship to the settlers themselves: "[Its] heterogeneous whole has an indisputable homogeneity that defies logic and triumphs over cross currents and contradictions," Pond offered.[36] Hull-House was built through repetition and iteration; neither objects nor subjects were fixed. When Addams spoke of the architects "harmoniz[ing] everything," she was referring to the way they assisted in the constant reorganization of the programmatic and physical components of the settlement complex, rather than to a balancing of distinct and unequal parts.[37] Hull-House's "skin," the assemblage of Italianate Victorian, Prairie school, and Arts and Crafts architecture common during the time, belies the polymorphous program (Figure 1.8). Guy Szuberla described the house as functionalist architecture clothed in historicist iconography, "an embodiment of the complex of progressive ideals: commitment to both a planned future and a sentimentalized past."[38] Victorian architecture need not compel Victorian lifestyles or values, and women residents at Hull-House were clearly rejecting Victorian norms regarding how they should lead their own lives. Of the growth of the settlement over the years, Addams wrote, "[The architects] clothed in brick and mortar and made visible to the world that which we were trying to do."[39] In the end, the Hull-House Social Settlement sat in thirteen buildings on one and a half city blocks. All buildings served multiple constituencies over the course of a day or week, and new spaces could be carved out of old buildings to support changing programs. As Florence Kelley stated, "[An] enterprise, started in warm enthusiasm by a resident, goes on long after that resident has dropped it."[40]

Many of the programs and spaces that Hull-House provided involved the introduction of services and spaces absent in the industrial tenement districts at the turn of the century. Even before any physical expansions took place in the house, concerns over health and sanitation led to the early introduction of public bathrooms and the use of the kitchen to conduct cooking classes. Space in the house was used to create a public library and to provide locations for various socially driven clubs for children and adults. In this sense, the settlement was a space for social life that could not be accommodated in crowded tenement quarters. In many ways, the completed complex of buildings provided the middle-class American domestic spaces unavailable to immigrants.[41] It also demonstrated how these previously private activities were expanding into the burgeoning social sphere, where they came up against the dense and disorderly conditions of the industrial city.

Nearly every one of the thirteen buildings built by 1913 contained residential space of one kind or another, from single (or shared) dormlike rooms to apartments housing married couples and their children, intermingling public and private functions within each building (Figure 1.9). Almost no building was built without some housing facilities for the growing, but often transient, resident population. Helen Lefkowitz-Horowitz, a scholar of nineteenth-century college life, compared the settlement to early women's

FIGURE 1.8 *Entrance to the Hull-House Social Settlement in the 1890s, with the third-story addition to the original building and the new Mary Crane Nursery establishing an open courtyard facing Halsted Street. Courtesy of Jane Addams Memorial Collection (JAMC-0000-00135-0163), Special Collections, University of Illinois at Chicago Library.*

colleges: "Hull-House recreated this college world for adult women in the city. It took the form of a nineteenth-century women's dormitory," she wrote,[42] although analysis of her discussion of the house and its industrial setting demonstrates that this analogy is inadequate. The limits of her analogy to the dormitory/house model of places like Smith College become clearer when it is drawn out a little further. Certainly during the period from 1889 to 1893, when all the residents lived in Hull's original house, shared domestic duties (although with a housekeeper), and began to take meals together (a tradition that would continue so definitively that it would eventually require the building of a dining hall to accommodate meals), the house was very dormlike in character.[43] Yet from the beginning, the neighbors were invited in to partake in the social activities that constituted the "social settlement" and that distinguished it from the "university settlement" model. Urban domesticity was one of the key pedagogical purposes of the house.

On the other hand, Lefkowitz-Horowitz's understanding of the house as a dormitory allows us to reflect on questions of a campus within the city. What is Hull-House's campus if not the neighborhood in which it sat? Hull-House inverted nineteenth-century campus ideals by enlarging rather than restricting the degree of urban encounter. In effect, Hull-House was a rejection of the idea that pedagogical spaces should be set apart from the larger, more chaotic milieu. Its residents, whose relationship to their neighbors was pedagogical in intent, were also to gain in their own understanding of the space of the "immigrant colonies" and the conditions wrought by rapid industrialization and population growth. As we will see, this relationship would be essential to the settlement's research agenda, which began to take shape in the 1890s and had an impact on the buildings' and their residents' role in shaping the city through progressive reform. Even though Hull-House's pedagogical spaces were not directed toward higher education, other aspects of the work conducted from the house anticipated forms of research that would eventually become the domain of university professors and their students. What was first understood as college extension away from the space of the university and into the space of the city in settlements such as Toynbee Hall would eventually return to reside within the campus, particularly as the social sciences developed within the framework of the research university.

The "clothing" of Hull-House may have intimated the residential community within, but, as we have seen, the settlement's functions immediately expanded beyond that. As it grew through the accretion of purpose-built buildings, the once anomalous objectlike suburban-rural home was increasingly engaged with the buildings and street life surrounding it (Figure 1.10). The primary activities offered by the Hull-House Social Settlement in the early 1890s were educational, employing pedagogical approaches geared toward immigrants and their children. Many of the young women who joined this new social project, especially Ellen Gates Starr, who had first come to Chicago as a schoolteacher, saw it as an opportunity to rethink modes of education in the urban environment.[44] Early additions to the house reflected these concerns. The Butler Art Gallery (1890) provided space for arts education and exhibition. The Smith Building (1895) expanded the space available for the crèche and kindergarten, responding to an immediate need to provide activities for the children of working mothers. These two buildings

Modern research universities as they developed in the late nineteenth century, which will be more greatly discussed in chapter 2, were very much a product of modernization. Even though not all were associated with growing, modern cities, they nevertheless moved beyond parochial concerns to address themselves to larger national and international audiences. A number of these institutions were expansions and reorganizations of existing schools, but others, including the University of Chicago, were built literally from the ground up. They responded to the interests of the industrializing nation, allying themselves with "persons of wealth, social prestige, or political influence."[49] As John R. Thelin described in *A History of American Higher Education,* the ability to pay for these new institutions was provided by industry: "the discretionary wealth generated by American corporations and enterprises in the late nineteenth century."[50] Industrial and commercial wealth was reflected in philanthropic zeal that in turn had an impact on campus architecture. Thelin continued:

> The architectural paradox of the American university of this period is that the newer the campus was, the older it appeared to be. Thanks once again to the unprecedented wealth (and egos) of donors, the new universities were magnificent memorials that relied on historical revival forms to connect the present to the past. Improvements in technology, including reinforced concrete and eventually I-beam construction, made possible the erection of tall office buildings clothed in Gothic stone or colonial brick. Whether for municipal buildings or lecture halls, Americans took planning seriously. The task of the university-builders was comparable to designing a complete city.[51]

Schools established during the colonial period, such as Harvard and Yale, often had to negotiate massive campus expansions within already dense urban locations. In contrast, new purpose-built institutions such as Columbia University, which became a university and moved its campus to Morningside Heights in northern Manhattan in the late nineteenth century, and the University of Chicago, which purchased land at what was then the "edge" of the city, had the opportunity to build on fresh land awaiting urban expansion.

Building an entirely new campus in conjunction with a new or changed idea of the mission and organization of higher education allowed campus architects—an increasing number of whom were receiving professional educations—to articulate new spaces in which that education would take place and to take into account the increasing complexity of the programs they needed to house. Among the problems to be addressed was the need to unite the concerns of a research professoriate and graduate students with those of an American collegiate tradition focused on undergraduates living in residence. The architecture critic A. D. F. Hamlin wrote in 1903, "New buildings have become necessary simply because the new education demands resources and an equipment for which the old provision was utterly inadequate. A chapel and four recitation-rooms were all that was necessary for the college of 1803. The library was amply accommodated in one or two of the rooms in an adjacent dormitory."[52] As Paul Venable Turner would later state, describing the University of Chicago campus:

> Unlike the traditional American college, the new university required a great diversity of academic buildings and laboratories, separate dormitory areas for undergraduates and graduates (male and female), plus such facilities as a museum, research library, and gymnasium. Accommodating these functions in a unified design was not easy, and became one of the major problems in campus planning in the following years.[53]

Speaking of the great increase in university buildings and campuses nationwide, Hamlin noted the ways in which "the cosmopolitan and eclectic quality of our taste is fitly expressed in the variety of architectural style which these modern college buildings display." But he also found the late-Gothic style particularly well suited to new collegiate architecture, not only because of its reference to English institutional precedents but also because it readily lent itself "to the treatment of long ranges of buildings of moderate height" and permitted "a more picturesque variety of mass and sky-line than the Georgian, and the more stately Classic and Renaissance styles."[54] The University of Chicago campus that Cobb designed can be understood as a hybrid of these organizational systems and referential styles. The loose-fitting neo-Gothic, used on more sprawling nonurban campuses such as Princeton University, was compacted and constrained to fit within city blocks and structured to focus internally, such as at Columbia University, addressing similar conditions in New York. Yet while McKim, Mead & White's assemblage of neoclassical and Georgian buildings and symmetrical Beaux-Arts of the lessons. Urban historian Richard Wade, in speaking of reformers in general, wrote, "Their ultimate goal was the assimilation into the American social system of the slum-born youngster, scrubbed clean of his foreignness, indistinguishable from all other Americans, or rather, all other *white* Americans."[6] Practical housekeeping centers would teach the skills necessary to transform the immigrant districts according to developing national standards and commercial interests, while business leaders and government debated housing reform and the creation of model housing.

The Model Apartment House, a project announced in a *Chicago Tribune* article on April 26, 1901, and discussed and illustrated by Allen B. Pond in a *Brickbuilder* magazine article in 1902, was to be the most socially complex and controversial of Hull-House's combined educational and domestic projects. Designed to combine a nursery and kindergarten with an apartment house, it was to offer complete apartments to house working women with children. The building was designed to incorporate elements of tenement reform then circulating throughout American cities, in particular, cross-ventilation afforded by a courtyard configuration. Why the Model Apartment House did not come about in this form is contested.[7] When the building opened as the Mary Crane Nursery in 1908, its program was an expanded version of that previously provided at Hull-House, incorporating both classrooms for the children and classrooms for their mothers.

The Model Apartment House would have brought together two concerns of the residents: the need for the improvement of the tenement district through the reform of its architecture and the need for the improvement of the lives of those compelled to live within it. Reformers often elided the problems of habitation and inhabitants: both required study and education. The net result, however, went beyond the reform or domestication of new Americans; it extended out to the reform and domestication of the industrial city through both legislative lobbying and institutional initiatives. Hull-House combined its concerns for "Americanizing" immigrants with its concerns for "urbanizing" them, and broadened from there to civilizing and domesticating the city itself. "The public schools in the immigrant colonies deserve all the praise as Americanizing agencies which can be bestowed upon them."[8] For Addams and many other progressive reformers, assimilation was a means to avoid class and race (meant as ethnic) conflict. Although arguments for urban education began under leaders such as Horace Mann in the middle of the nineteenth century, they were extended and institutionalized by the end of the century.[9] Pragmatism, as developed by such psychologists and philosophers as William James, Charles S. Peirce, and John Dewey, would further link pluralism and social struggle to the context of the urban conflicts of the industrial city.[10]

Schools, playgrounds, and field houses were all pedagogical spaces, and they performed best when they acted together. Dewey articulated these ideas when he advocated for schools to be conceived as social centers as the schoolhouse expanded to meet the demands of mass education: "The pressing thing, the significant thing, is really to make the school a social center; that is a matter of practice, not of theory. Just what to do to make the schoolhouse a center of full and adequate social service, to bring it completely into the current of social life" would be an important focus of progressive education.[11] In this formulation, the public school became more than the space for the education, socialization, and ultimate assimilation of the immigrant child. It was to be a space for adult extension classes (college classes for people not enrolled as regular students), language education, amusement, and recreation. It was a space of social exchange directly extended from the social settlement:

> What we want is to see the school, every public school, doing something of the same sort of work that is now done by a settlement or two scattered at wide distances thru the city. And we all know that the work of such an institution as Hull-House has been primarily, not that of conveying intellectual instruction, but of being a social clearing-house.[12]

Social settlements may have helped initiate the public library, playground, and kindergarten movements, and they may have provided spaces for social clubs, home economics classes, and English instruction, but they were private institutions of limited breadth and reach. The progressive reform and education movements sought to shift these responsibilities into the public domain by making them a responsibility of the government. As they did so, the role of the social settlement would change. Nonetheless, it remained an important social and socialization instrument for another half century.

In marked contrast—although not without great overlap in intent—to the urban institutions established through progressive reform was Burnham and Bennett's monumental and far-reaching *Plan of Chicago* of 1909 (Figure 2.1). The plan was a complex document of text and images that established a commercial and civic logic for a reenvisioning of Chicago within its

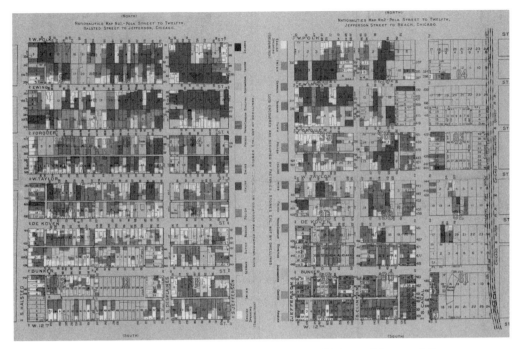

FIGURE 2.2 *Portion of the Nationalities Map from* Hull-House Maps and Papers *illustrating the diversity of ethnic and racial groups throughout the settlement neighborhood. Courtesy of Special Collections, University of Illinois at Chicago Library.*

On the other hand, *Hull-House Maps and Papers* was conceived not as a "scientific" project but as an "activist" project. Kathryn Kish Sklar, through her biography of Florence Kelley and explorations of the role of social science in the settlement movement, did much to advance a theory of the "precocious" nature of Hull-House's use of geography in social analysis.[23] Kelley began her investigations in Chicago studying women's working conditions, which resulted in a report on "the sweating system" and ultimately in her position as the first chief factory inspector for the state of Illinois.[24] As Sklar noted, Kelley's influence on Addams at Hull-House was to "[redirect] the settlement's activities away from neighborly aid and toward larger issues of public policy."[25] In the end, both activities would continue side by side.

The survey, maps, and analyses conducted by Kelley, Hull-House residents, and additional workers were clearly constructive, but they were also instructive, setting a standard for future sociological study of urban environments in general and of immigrant neighborhoods in particular.

Although both Addams and Kelley saw the important role of the settlement in social reform, their politics, conceptual frameworks, and methodologies were different. Kelley had advocated early on for the role of women in social science, while Addams wrote in the introduction to the book, "[The] energies [of Hull-House residents] have been chiefly directed not toward sociological investigation, but to constructive work."[26] In this respect, *Hull-House Maps and Papers* is an outgrowth of the hybrid milieu of Hull-House as a late-nineteenth-century social space. It also reflects a burgeoning generational tension in the concerns of individual residents and the focus of their projects:

> Women's settlements and other women's organisations enabled a
> generation of college-trained women to forge lifelong commitments
> to social science based reform organisations that were independent
> of the political climate in universities. These same organisations
> also channeled women's energies deeper in gender-specific topics
> and issues.[27]

Despite the fact that Addams resisted professionalization of the settlement in the same way she resisted institutionalization, many female residents were or became professionals, some directly involved with universities. However, although Addams worked in a network that included the University of Chicago faculty and other academics from around the nation, she consistently resisted attempts to bring Hull-House under the aegis of the university as part of her argument for understanding the social settlement as a house rather than as an institution committed to its neighbors, even as it undertook larger projects for urban reform. Hull-House residents brought legitimacy to the study of urban life, not just its monuments and institutions, by focusing on the quotidian as both unchanging and yet completely provisional. In the long run, much of the long-term impact of the settlement movement was a result of the extent to which individual settlement residents became involved in developing city and state social agencies, federal bureaus, and university programs.

The City as Laboratory

The University of Chicago exemplified the new urban university that arose in the late nineteenth century. Conditions in Chicago were particularly well suited to such an institution. The industrial city required new professionals and bureaucratic expertise to keep it running. It needed scientists and social scientists to expand knowledge regarding urban conditions. And as we have seen, those who had earned their wealth from the industrialization of the city were willing to fund such an institution for reasons both practical and egotistical. These conditions intersected well with changes in higher education that were taking place nationwide.

There exists a vast literature on the development of higher education in the United States. Although authors disagree on which institutions first exhibited signs of the emerging trend toward research-based knowledge as the intellectual core of the university, which institutions best exemplified its traits, and what distinguished a college from a university, all agree that the transformation took place between the end of the Civil War and the beginning of World War I, with particular emphasis in the twenty years bracketing 1900, the year the American Association of Universities was founded with the intention of developing policies on the granting of graduate degrees.[28] The historian of higher education Roger L. Geiger found a parallelism between national institutions in general and higher education in particular: both were evolving "from small localized concerns with parochial interests and clienteles into bureaucratic organizations integrated with national communications networks."[29] The hallmark of the university of the late nineteenth and early twentieth centuries was a shift toward a concern with the production of knowledge. The seeds for this movement were sown in the middle of the nineteenth century when, Geiger noted, reform-minded educators started advocating for an increasing emphasis on the development of research, focusing on the need for scientific study and institutionalized practical training. At the same time, scholars began to lobby for opportunities for advanced studies in the United States similar to what was becoming available in European universities.[30] Americans traveling to Europe for such education, especially those who studied in the new German universities exemplified by the University of Berlin, founded by Wilhelm von Humboldt in 1810, would bring the disciplinary structure, teaching methods, and research focus of these institutions back to the United States. In the years immediately following the Civil War, the land-grant colleges established under the Morrill Act (1862) began to expand the scope of higher education and make it more commonly available. Yet the methodology of their funding, their orientation toward "agriculture and the mechanic arts," and their tendency to be located in agricultural rather than urban environments meant that they could not directly take up the concerns of industrialization, and they tended toward practical concerns over more universal ideas of knowledge production. This would not change until the second Morrill Act, of 1890, which, along with subsequent federal legislation, expanded funding for applied research.[31]

In the United States in the late nineteenth century, the specialized research focus of the European universities intersected with the increasing liberalization and secularization of the collegiate curriculum, best exemplified by Charles W. Eliot's introduction of the elective system at Harvard in 1869. Although some new universities, notably Johns Hopkins, founded in 1876, would for a number of years devote themselves exclusively to graduate study, most of the new or expanding institutions would strike an uneasy balance between undergraduate liberal arts education and research interests. Even with regard to research, two sometimes competing interests could be found: the specialization of knowledge and with it practical and professional education as it might address the needs of an industrial society, on the one hand, and a "climate of abstract investigation" valorizing objective and experimental methodologies, on the other.[32] "Pure science" would become the basis for the methodologies of emerging disciplines in the "social" sciences, fields that studied human and social organization. Chief among these was sociology, applicable to the study of the structure of modern social formation.

Given the location, foundation, and scientific undercurrent of the University of Chicago, it is not surprising to find that the study of the city would be an early focus of its faculty:

> [William Rainey] Harper and [Harry Pratt Judson, his successor], like the leaders of other universities in large cities, made a virtue of their urban locations. Harper insisted that "urban universities are in the truest sense national universities" because "the great cities represented the national life in its fullness and its variety." Judson went further, insisting that the service responsibilities of the urban university should be applied primarily to the city itself:
> "In the great city with its crowded population the limits of the university duties are to be conceived as coterminous with the limits of the city itself. In other words, the university should not be content with the discovery only of scientific truth, which may have most direct bearing upon the city life, but should be especially industri-

ous in the investigation and dissemination of such forms of truth as are directly related to the city."[33]

Among the first faculty members hired by Harper was Albion Small, who founded the first American department of sociology at the University of Chicago in 1892. Small was a product of the modern university, having studied in Germany at the universities in Leipzig and Berlin and having received his Ph.D. from Johns Hopkins, but he was also a Baptist minister. In this way he exemplified the intersection of research and reform interests still present within university research at the turn of the century. Under Small's leadership, Chicago would become a center for the development of the discipline as he founded its first professional journal, wrote its earliest textbooks, and educated or hired the individuals who would orient the "Chicago school of sociology" toward the study of urban social organization.

The new universities were not only centers for professional scholars and scientists; they also served society by creating a professional culture based on rationality, expertise, training, and authority. Historian Burton Bledstein wrote, "Americans lacked tradition as a source of authority, but they did not lack 'science.' It was the primary function of American universities to render universal scientific standards credible to the public."[34] Not only modern medicine, law, and architecture but also planning, business management, engineering, accounting, social work, teaching, and government organization would be codified and institutionalized during this period, as would the methods by which one would have access to these professions.

If research were to become the defining feature of the modern university, what did this mean with regard to urban research? Here the University of Chicago was to play a singular role:

Chicago is an ideal setting for a case study of professors' impact on urban policy in these years. The nation's second largest city, it attracted national attention for the magnitude of its social ills but also for the dynamism of its reform movement. Many of the nation's most important reform leaders lived in the city of Jane Addams, and what happened in Chicago had ramifications for the rest of the nation. The University of Chicago was founded at the very beginning of a period of nationwide reform. From the start, it was a full-fledged graduate university, emphasizing scholarly research and graduate teaching.[35]

Yet although Hull-House benefited from its informal relationships with the University of Chicago faculty, it was increasingly marginalized by them. At the University of Chicago, the work spearheaded by the social settlements would bifurcate into two distinct areas of training and expertise: social work and urban sociology. Sociology would be formulated as a scientific discipline, alongside which social work would develop as a profession. Each derived from the transient and conflict-ridden conditions of life in the industrial city, so well described in *Hull-House Maps and Papers*.

Social work would emerge as a profession through the work of Hull-House residents Julia C. Lathrop, Edith Abbott, and Sophonisba P. Breckinridge, but under the auspices of the University of Chicago. With Graham Taylor and Charles R. Henderson, Lathrop began to offer training courses through the University of Chicago extension service. Then, because of financial disagreements within the university, she helped establish and lead the independent Chicago School of Civics and Philanthropy. Here she hired Abbott and Breckinridge to assist her. These two women represented a new generation; both held Ph.D.'s in economics from the University of Chicago and had worked within its culture. They felt that only professionally educated individuals had the knowledge and skill appropriate to proper social research, advocacy, policy making, and work.

> Breckinridge and Abbott, nearly alone among the founders of academic social work, urged rigorous academic training, preferably on the graduate level, to enable social workers to conduct research on social problems and contribute to their remedy as well as to provide direct services to the needy. In short, they thought social work should become the science of social policy, which applied the most advanced knowledge and research to concrete human problems by combining academic work and fieldwork. Such an ideal, they believed, could best be realized within a university and not, as almost everyone else in the field insisted, in an independent, vocationally-oriented school.[36]

Lathrop left the Chicago School of Civics and Philanthropy in 1913 to head up the new Children's Bureau in Washington, D.C. Under the leadership of Abbott and Breckinridge, the school reunited with the University of Chicago in 1920 to become the School of Social Service Administration. Although closely affiliated with Hull-House and the University of Chicago Settlement, these women successfully brought social work into being as a professional, rather than a philanthropic, activity. As a result, many future Hull-House residents and staff would come to the settlement trained as social workers.

Despite advocacy for careful and detailed urban research, exemplified by Abbott's book *The Tenements of Chicago, 1908–1935,* the School of Social Service Administration was eclipsed by the Department of Sociology in the early decades of the twentieth century.[37] Urban sociology, particularly under the auspices of Small's successors, including Robert E. Park, Ernest W. Burgess, Lewis Wirth, and later Donald J. Bogue, would become the leading field in the utilization of the social survey to develop theories of urban transformation. During the first half of the twentieth century, the Chicago school of sociology used the sociological study of Chicago, understood as *the* American city, as a paradigm for modern—urban—social theory throughout the United States. In his reflections on the origins of the Department of Sociology, Burgess credited Hull-House with carrying out the first "field studies" in Chicago: "If you go back as far as 1895 in the Hull-House Papers, you will find urban studies. It would be correct to say that systematic urban studies in Chicago began with these Hull-House studies." He also credited Abbott and Breckinridge for their studies beginning as early as 1908.[38] Numerous writings have addressed the way this bifurcation reflected gender relationships within the University of Chicago—women in charge of teaching and training for service professions, men in control of research and theoretical explication.[39] Space does not allow for a detailed explication of this process. Of interest to this study is the way urban sociology would stake its claim as a *science,* with the city as its *laboratory* for the development of theories of social transformation.

In their famous anthology *The City* (1925), Park, Burgess, and their colleagues set out to provide an analysis of the modern city. Here, not only would the methodologies reflect developing scientific principles, but the city would be understood as a topic of science, as a distinct form of social relationship, a disturbed ecology brought about by change, mobility, and overstimulation. Although they recognized the importance of the social settlements, they argued that sociology was more capable of solving urban ills; Burgess wrote, "The task of the sociologist is twofold: to secure the cooperation of specialists in the university and of the departments of state and to organize the community for self-investigation under expert direction."[40] He relegated the social settlement to the realm of sentiment, claiming expertise for the university alone. Park recognized the role of the social settlements for "certain methods and a technique for stimulating and controlling local communities." Reflecting the scientific underpinnings of modern sociology, Park described the city as a "laboratory or clinic in which human nature and social processes may be conveniently and profitably studied."[41] Like the founders of Hull-House, he believed that the problems of particular urban areas were based on the exigencies of industrial phenomena that appeared to affect some social groups more than others; however, urban sociologists—at that time—did not think it appropriate or necessary to live among their study subjects to do their research. Nor was the goal of their research to work directly within those communities to resolve their problems or to advocate for urban reform. They sought a more detached, objective perspective. The response of urban sociologists was to understand what they referred to as the ecological basis of new urban phenomena. Whereas social settlements studied the "factors" at work in their neighborhoods, the urban sociologists studied the "forces." As the sociologist Sudhir Venkatesh observed, the "conceptualization of how cities grow actually deemphasized the role of politics and planned intervention."[42] Burgess held that "if neighborhood work can have a scientific basis, it is because there are social forces in community life—forces like geographical conditions, human wishes, community consciousness—that can be studied, described, analyzed, and ultimately measured."[43] If it can be said that the social settlement worked in the tight space left by the collapse of the boundary between public and private, then the urban sociologists saw that collapse as a threat to both private life and the public realm, classifying its causes and professionalizing and legislating responses.

The essays and case studies in *The City* built an argument for linking human behavior to an urban ecology that could be described through processes of extension and succession, concentration and decentralization (Figure 2.3). One can think of urban growth "as a resultant of organization and disorganization analogous to the anabolic and katabolic processes of metabolism in the body," Burgess wrote.[44] The applicability of the Chicago school's theories to Chicago is not speculative but direct, as, working to establish themselves as scientists, urban sociologists utilized the urban laboratory of Chicago's "zone in transition"—the immigrant ghettos surrounding the loop—and the so-called Black Belt of the South Side to develop and test their hypotheses, which would be applied at a national scale. There is no question that the work of Chicago's sociologists would affect local and national policies and legislation, just as Hull-House's research influenced urban reform. The distinguishing features were methodological and, to a certain degree, spatial. Social workers conducted studies within their neighborhoods in order to improve the conditions in those communities, while their colleagues, the sociologists, were looking to develop theories to explain the patterns and processes they observed in the same communities.

The Chicago school's analytic framework and the language it used to bring its theories to a larger public audience in the 1920s and 1930s set the stage for further analogies and analytic action. If a city was analogous to a human or corporate body it could grow, but it could also deteriorate, degrade, and become diseased. More specifically, it could become "blighted." Blight is a parasite; it comes from an outside source, often unknown, and causes disease and decay. The usefulness, power, and longevity of this word as applied to urban environments cannot be ignored. The development of the concept of "blight" brought with it the possibility of "renewal" through proper management and restoration. Blight was understood to be more than a physical characteristic of an environment; for many it also implied the character traits of a specific race, class, or ethnicity, whose members became its identifiers: "Slums are a problem or a threat in many cities, but those of Chicago—23 festering, proliferating square miles aswarm with 800,000 human beings—are the nation's most dramatic case of municipal decay," wrote *Life* magazine.[45] Blight in this view is a state and a process, a historical devolution, from a previously balanced state, a state prior to the effects of modernity. Blight can be prevented, but when necessary, it can be removed: "It can be cured by radium if taken in time, but after it has gotten to a certain stage, it infects the body politic, and the only cure for it is to cut with the surgeon's knife."[46] Eventually, the analogies promulgated in the work of the Chicago school of sociology faculty in the 1920s and 1930s would begin to affect the physical form of Chicago through the auspices of national calls for urban renewal.

Important studies on race and ethnicity, politics, geography, juvenile delinquency, hobos, and homosexuality, among other topics, would emerge through graduate dissertations and faculty articles and monographs, each developed from detailed case studies of conditions in Chicago between World Wars I and II. Many were funded by Chicago-based foundations and philanthropic organizations. In "Chicago's Pragmatic Planners," Venkatesh has carefully elaborated how, despite their claims to objectivity and their tangential role in urban planning, Chicago's social scientists' "descriptive" techniques would have "prescriptive" implications.[47] An important outcome

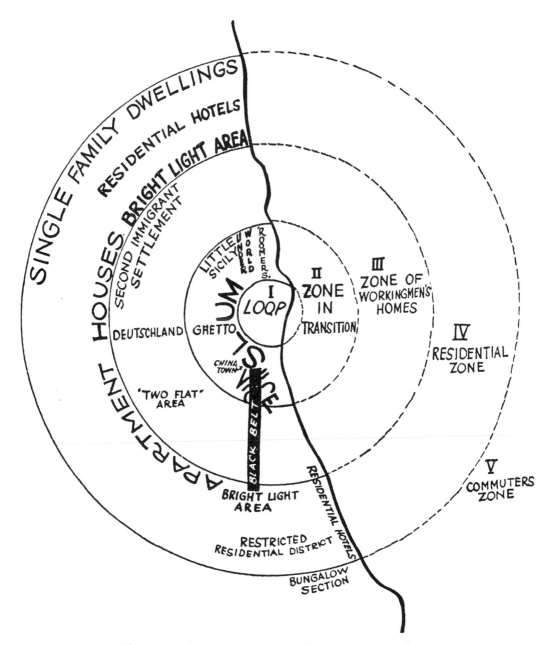

FIGURE 2.3 *Chicago school of sociology diagram illustrating the development of the idea of "natural areas" based on the theory of extension and succession in Chicago in the early twentieth century. Ernest W. Burgess, "The Growth of the City," in* The City, *ed. Robert E. Park, Ernest W. Burgess, and Roderick D. McKenzie (1925; repr., University of Chicago Press, 1967). Courtesy of the University of Chicago Press.*

of this work, the interdisciplinary Local Community Research Committee, worked to organize and compile the great variety of urban research coming from field-studies courses and community surveys. *The Local Community Fact Book* was founded in 1938 and still exists today. After World War II, sociological research at the University of Chicago was organized under the Chicago Community Inventory with the aim of providing an information resource on the Chicago metropolitan area, and under the Community and Family Study Center to conduct research on and experiments around family life in the city. The resulting mappings and technical surveys of urban space and social relations would shape how Chicagoans understood their city and how they would reorganize it to meet the needs of the twentieth century. Blight—its prevention and its cure through the auspices of urban renewal—would help frame and promote the next phase of urban transformation. In particular, urban renewal would provide the impetus and the methodology for expanding the space of higher education in the city in the postwar period.

also become important elements in politicians' and civic leaders' plans to re-shape the city. Even as universities were becoming more wary of their urban environments, often seeking to flee from them, urban leaders were looking for more ways to encourage their growth and using them as anchor institutions for urban renewal.

Urban Renewal and Chicago's Universities

Urban renewal played a key role in the expansion of higher education, providing the funds, lands, and mechanisms through which colleges and universities could be built or grown in situ. In Chicago, for example, the Illinois Institute of Technology (IIT) was established on "blighted" land in the Black Belt, and the location of the University of Illinois at Chicago Circle (UICC) would come about through changes in urban renewal policies developed at the University of Chicago.[11] Chicago presents an interesting case study because much of what was later codified as urban renewal was first "tested" in the city's own programs, some prior to World War II.[12] And in Chicago we can see the way modern urban design conjoined with the politics of urban renewal to produce distinctive campus forms.

Under the leadership of Mayor Richard J. Daley (1955–1976), urban renewal would begin to take place at a scale and speed unmatched in any other American city, with the possible exception of New York City. Daley played a pivotal role in Chicago's postwar redevelopment because, as a result of his participation in national Democratic politics, he brought to the city's specific experience of the decline of heavy industry and the decentralization of cities an ability to obtain federal urban renewal funding. Daley converted the federal dollars into major public works projects—generally allied with business interests—in order to recentralize the city economically, politically, and physically. These developments were a double-edged sword. Although they assisted in buffering against, even though not stemming, the tide of white, middle-class residents and businesses moving out of the city, much of the work resulted in the neglect and continued decline of Chicago's neighborhoods, as slum clearance often led to the wholesale demolition of communities.

Daley implemented and oversaw the city's postwar transformation in its initial, often violent, moves from an industrial to a postindustrial city.[13] He exerted almost panoptic control over "Chicagoland." Born into the strict and insular Irish-Catholic neighborhood of Bridgeport in Chicago, Daley was a product of Chicago's entrenched neighborhood system of the late nineteenth and early twentieth centuries. But he became mayor as this system was beginning to unravel, during the city's restructuring from a dense modern city to a distributed regional city. Chicago, like many American cities, was significantly altered by new federal interstate highways, which were initially designed to speed traffic around densely developed parts of the country, and by large high-rise public housing projects that all but obliterated nineteenth-century neighborhoods. Among the projects that can be attributed to his administration are the nation's largest collection of public housing projects; the Kennedy, Dan Ryan, Eisenhower, and Stevenson expressways; O'Hare International Airport; extension of the mass transportation system to the airports; McCormick Place Convention Center; and the Federal Center building complex. An equally important component of his strategy for maintaining Chicago's centrality in its metropolitan region was the expansion of opportunities for higher education within the city. The UICC campus became the capstone project for this education plan as Daley enabled this initiative through funding and policies that were directly connected to the city's urban renewal programs, but it was not alone in reaping the rewards of federal dollars directed to the city and through it to public and private urban institutions. Federal urban renewal funding and legislation would be used to sponsor the campus within the city and, in turn, would implicate it in the urban spatial transformations that took place in the middle of the twentieth century.[14]

While residential urban renewal projects and the federal interstate system were reconfiguring the urban landscapes surrounding the city's center, Daley's planners laid out plans for the redevelopment of the Central Area of Chicago (CAC), intending to shore up the increasingly blighted Loop—the city's dense downtown business and retail district—through the appropriation and redesignation of industrial land and residential districts surrounding the downtown. One key to the proposals was the rethinking of the city's transportation infrastructure: the consolidation of the city's tangled web of railroads, the construction of new airports, the extension of new highways, and the rerouting of Lake Shore Drive, the major artery along the Lake Michigan waterfront. Another important element was the reorganization of urban land. Under the leadership of Ira J. Bach, the Chicago Plan Commission mapped out over thirty discrete projects, all designed to stem blight, increase land values, develop new middle-class housing, and encourage businesses and cultural institutions to remain in the city. Presented in August 1958, the proposal was clearly designed to retain Chicago's primary status in its rapidly expanding urban region. The new expressways—the Congress, Northwest, and South (later renamed the Eisenhower, Kennedy, and Dan Ryan, respectively)—were the nexus of the plan, converging on what was to become the Chicago Circle interchange, the focus of Daley's new city. In the tradition of the *Plan of Chicago*, the development plan provided not only maps and a text but also extensive architectural renderings of projects proposed by this new urbanism.

A proposal for the Chicago campus of the University of Illinois (Figure 3.1) makes a significant appearance in this plan.[15] In the 1950s, as the University of Illinois began to explore how to accommodate baby-boom students, it began to explore ways to expand its presence in and around Chicago. While the university's board of trustees and the Real Estate Research Corporation (RERC) scanned the region and the city for suitable sites, Daley and Bach were envisioning the university not as a regional asset but as an opportunity to replace the city's declining industrial network, centered south of the Loop, with a new educational–cultural complex running south from Congress Street to Fourteenth Street and west from State Street to the Chicago River. Their plan proposed new middle- and upper-income high-rise housing along the east side of State Street:

> The location is also highly desirable for the University and its students. It is near the Art Institute, the Crerar Library and Chicago Public Library, the Museum of Natural History, the Planetarium, and the recreation facilities of Soldier Field, Grant Park, and Lake Michigan. It is also close to opportunities for part-time student employment. . . . In this site, the University would be accessible to students and faculty and University employees living throughout the entire Metropolitan Area. All routes of the expressway system and the suburban railroad system converge here, and all existing rapid transit lines immediately adjoin the site. With the development of the Wells Street subway, another route would directly serve the University.[16]

Indeed, the drawing of the proposed campus shows State Street as a boulevard flanked on the east by high-rise housing (replete with gardens in the air) and on the west by low-rise buildings, parking, and open spaces, in the idiom of a modernist corporate office park. An elevated east–west roadway runs through the image. Ultimately, the campus would not be located where the plan recommended, but other features of the plan suggested sites that would later come into play.

FIGURE 3.1 *Rendering of city of Chicago proposal to locate the University of Illinois on land owned by the railroads along State Street south of the Loop in the mid-1950s. Image looking north with the Congress Expressway and the Loop in the distance and proposed new middle-class housing along the east side of the street.* Chicago Department of City Planning, Development Plan for the Central Area of Chicago, August 1958, *Department of City Planning, Ira J. Bach, Commissioner.*

The 1958 plan also offered proposals for 237 acres of the Near West Side southwest of the proposed interchange, comprising the Community Conservation Board's Near West Side project, which focused on the rehabilitation of the existing neighborhood; five Chicago Housing Authority (CHA) projects (several of which were already built); and two Chicago Land Clearance Commission (CLCC) projects totaling fifty-five acres and known as the Harrison–Halsted Project, the neighborhood immediately surrounding Hull-House (Figure 3.2):

> It will include [a] new multi-family residential development and a limited amount of new commercial development. Existing sound commercial and industrial structures at the eastern end of the project are to be retained. The Thirteenth and Blue Island project,

covering four acres, will provide a local shopping center for the residential area surrounding it.[17]

By 1961 these fifty-five acres would be among the most contested in the city, as plans for new housing would be abandoned for the new UICC campus on the site.[18]

Although Daley's plans for a new University of Illinois campus in Chicago clearly articulated the campus's potential to redevelop the blighted South Loop and restore its commercial base, equally important were the advantages the campus would gain through its proximity to downtown. Accessibility was critical, but so were the city's cultural amenities and employment opportunities. The city was to provide the extended campus for the university. This concept of an urban campus envisioned a relationship between the development and dispersal of the university's knowledge and the city's cultural, social, and economic opportunities and resources.

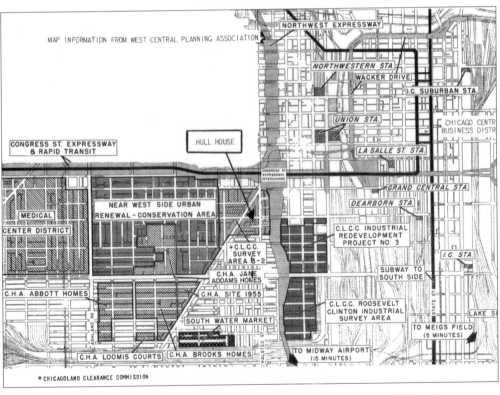

FIGURE 3.2 *Plan indicating the Chicago Land Clearance Commission designations on the Near West Side; note the location of Hull-House. Chicago Land Clearance Commission.*

The Modern Campus and Urban Renewal

Convincing the University of Illinois board of trustees to build their new campus in the center of Chicago was the ongoing focus of Mayor Daley's program for higher education as it related to urban renewal, but two additional institutions, IIT and the University of Chicago, were equally important in establishing a link between the concerns of pedagogical institutions and their impact on post–World War II Chicago. At IIT, Ludwig Mies van der Rohe, a leading German architect, brought European modernist architecture and planning to the design of a new campus on Chicago's South Side. IIT served as a prototype for the design of modern institutions within the postwar urban landscape, and perhaps the environment to be most affected by it would be the Chicago neighborhoods surrounding it. The cloistered University of Chicago also underwent expansion in the middle of the century, but that expansion was more in keeping with the university's neo-Gothic traditions. Its impact was less on urban form than on how urban renewal policy would be implemented in an attempt to strengthen urban institutions within the context of the deteriorated nineteenth-century urban fabric.

With the exception of the University of Virginia, no campus in America is as linked to its architect as Chicago's IIT is to Mies van der Rohe. Appointed in 1938 as director of the architecture school at the Armour Institute of Technology (which would become the Illinois Institute of Technology in 1940), Mies, like Thomas Jefferson, designed his campus to demonstrate principles of architecture and urbanism that would form the core of new ways of teaching and conceiving American space:

> Unlike Jefferson's Neoclassical campus set amid the rolling, verdant landscape of eighteenth-century Virginia and devoted to the traditional educational principles of the Enlightenment, Mies was called upon to insert a modern campus for an evolving institution devoted to technological education in the flatlands of the dense urban slums of Chicago's Near South Side, and to design buildings that could accommodate a growing emphasis on scientific research.[19]

Whereas Jefferson looked to Europe in designing buildings that would demonstrate Enlightenment architecture, and in so doing hoped to instill students with reverence for Enlightenment principles of reason and individualism, Mies set about to organize the IIT campus using design principles he had been developing in Europe between World War I and World War II, hoping to use the campus as a demonstration of new ways of conceiving urban space. Additionally, each architect imported examples of contemporary European architecture to serve as models for their students to learn from and execute. Although Mies came up against urban conditions only partially under architects' control, to a large extent he succeeded in designing a campus that utilized new materials and technology, functional rationalization of building types, and an internal organization that opened campus spaces to the city as a whole. His campus has become part of the legacy of the remaking of American cities through modern urban design principles and urban policies that would be promoted by urban renewal planners.

Like some of Chicago's early experiments with public housing, the design of the IIT campus advanced ideas that would later be incorporated into state and federal legislation that would lead to the large-scale urban renewal of major portions of Chicago's South Side in the 1950s. According to architectural theorist Sarah Whiting, "While a sincere desire to ameliorate slum conditions was the impetus behind the drive for urban renewal, a genuine fear that this moral underbelly, combined with the deterioration of the area's building stock, would multiply and spread across Chicago provided the immediate impetus to act."[20] These concerns for the area as a whole were encapsulated into the campus site. The institute, first through individual land purchases and then through legislation, was able to acquire property to house its core academic activities and residential needs and to protect its boundaries. As Whiting detailed, this expansion was enabled by the physical decline of the neighborhood, which made IIT's land relatively valueless and, consequently, made land acquisition inexpensive as the institute established itself at the northern edge of what would become the largest clearing for urban renewal in the United States.[21]

With the exception of the original Armour Institute buildings, all the land earmarked for the IIT campus was cleared of its buildings. "What could be called 'inner-city landfill,' or land acquisition, was the keystone to all development on the Near South Side, for every project within the plan depended on a tabula rasa in order to construct its envisioned campus."[22] Because the entire area was deemed to be "blighted," all "renewal" was predicated on the "clearance" of anything preexisting on the site. The principles undergirding the design, if not the final effect, are exemplified in an iconic image published in *Architectural Forum* magazine in 1942 (updated in 1947) in which a model of the campus is collaged onto a photograph of the neighborhood

(Figure 3.3). The aging, dense fabric of the neighborhood stands in stark contrast to the new ground plane of the campus with its assemblage of large glass-and-steel buildings.

Mies's design for IIT intentionally inverted both the fabric of the nineteenth-century city and the quadrangular, neo-Gothic campus of the University of Chicago. His buildings acknowledge neither the street nor the street wall created by the city's organization by block and lot. Instead, the campus is an assemblage of discrete buildings that take their positions relative to one another. Phyllis Lambert wrote of the design development as it stood in 1939:

> This sketch . . . establishes the sense of inward orientation that Mies would favor for the IIT campus, insofar as it would be necessary to enter into the campus in order to gain access to the buildings. The space he eventually created would nonetheless be uniquely permeable, standing in stark contrast to the gated enclave of the typical North American university campus.[23]

The academic campus continued the logic of the nineteenth-century street grid and yet countered it through an internally directed sequence of overlapping spaces:

> Mies's campus plan engendered a new conceptual-spatial model for the American city . . . conforming to the existing street grid but breaking up the solid wall of buildings along the street edge. . . . While Mies established a major central greensward space, it flowed like water around stones into the open and compressed spaces created by buildings sliding past one another.[24]

Within the canon of modern architecture, Mies is best known as an architect of steel and glass, of singular objects and universal space, perhaps the best known of which is Crown Hall, the School of Architecture at IIT. Yet Whiting, in her detailed analysis of the development of the campus and its role in the further development of Chicago's South Side into a collection of superblocks of urban institutions and public housing—"campuses"—has noted that the area plan that emerged from this work "was subsequently envisioned as a viable prototype for rescuing the postwar American city."[25] Three elements of the IIT campus would become the norm in American urban design in the

described as a process of "neighborhood succession" was now commonly understood as "racial succession," so that a neighborhood experiencing an in-migration of African Americans, prolonged neglect, and overcrowding would be understood to be experiencing "blight," reflecting the clear racial dynamics at play in urban renewal.[33]

Urban renewal in the areas surrounding the University of Chicago in the middle of the twentieth century is an example of the broad-stroke approach taken by planners looking to restore "blighted" parts of the American cities. The slum-clearance approach to blight had little nostalgia for the late-nineteenth- and early-twentieth-century city, particularly neighborhoods that had served as points of entry for European immigrants or Chicago's segregated Black Belt. Looking retrospectively at the relationship of preservation, urban renewal, and race in Chicago in the middle of the twentieth century, architectural historian Daniel Bluestone noted, "The broader planning effort aimed to 'preserve' the university's community as a viable middle-class housing area by demolishing the buildings that housed poor, working-class, and largely African-American residents."[34] Ironically, only several decades later, preservation has become the centerpiece of much urban stabilization as "revival" and "restoration" have replaced "renewal" as the focus of many city and neighborhood planning departments.

In the 1950s, the popular press portrayed Chicago as both America's most blighted city and the city most committed to removing blight through urban renewal. In a sidebar accompanying a 1955 *Life* article focusing on the "encroaching menace" of slums, filled with images of Chicago's "teaming and infested world," "Slum Fighter Levi," as Julian Levi, executive director of the SECC was nicknamed, offered recommendations for what urban residents should do: "If your neighborhood is changing, if it is slipping toward overcrowded rooming houses, hole-in-the-wall businesses and an unstable, transient population; if your crime and delinquency rates are rising and your garbage collection standards falling—then you must act quickly and boldly to save your neighborhood from becoming a slum." He continued, "The slum warnings are on every street corner in our communities of Hyde Park and Kenwood. But we have been bold and persistent and I believe we have found the answer. It is called 'Urban Renewal.'"[35] Through the auspices of SECC and HPKCC, the communities around the University of Chicago became the site of an urban renewal demonstration project (Figure 3.4). Levi's local work began to have national impact when he lobbied for the changes to the Federal Housing Act (FHA) discussed below. Levi explained the need for such changes:

Universities and colleges are not civic betterment associations. Their missions—teaching, training, research, and the extension of man's knowledge about himself and his universe—should not be diverted into operations in city planning and redevelopment *unless these diversions are essential to the fulfillment of the primary missions.* It is, however, a tragic fact that these efforts are today essential to the ability of the institutions to fulfill their primary responsibilities. [Emphasis added][36]

This local activity had far-reaching consequences for national trends in urban renewal as landlocked urban campuses experiencing rapid growth in their student populations had to contend with the context of their declining neighborhoods. The *New York Times* stated the problem bluntly: "For the institutions it is a two-front war: They must contend with the lack of space in a crowded setting; and they must halt the encroachment of slums which turn the lack of space for expansion into a straightjacket of physical danger."[37] In a 1960 *Architectural Record* report on urban renewal in Hyde Park–Kenwood, the University of Chicago chancellor Lawrence A. Kimpton was quoted as saying, "We are fighting for our lives—we simply cannot operate in a slum area."[38] Throughout the 1950s, educational institutions worked in piecemeal fashion to purchase and rehabilitate buildings in their neighborhoods, but they also assisted in the selection of buildings to be demolished and in decisions on where to locate new buildings. In Chicago, these practices attenuated existing segregation (which the university had supported until restrictive covenants were outlawed in 1948) through the building of new public housing for low-income (largely African American) residents and private housing for middle- and upper-income (largely white) residents.

At the same time, many urban schools began to look for more coherent ways to expand into and control their neighborhoods. The *New York Times* reported that the presidents of Harvard, Columbia, the University of Pennsylvania, Yale, and the Massachusetts Institute of Technology (MIT) met in 1957 to look at conditions surrounding several urban campuses. These institutions also urged the federal government to enact legislation on their behalf. In 1959 the passage of Section 112 of the FHA of 1949 made it possible to use federal aid for "urban renewal areas involving colleges and universities."[39] Levi, using his own experiences at the University of Chicago, helped frame the new section, which also allowed cities to claim university funds used in this manner as part of their contribution to overall urban renewal efforts

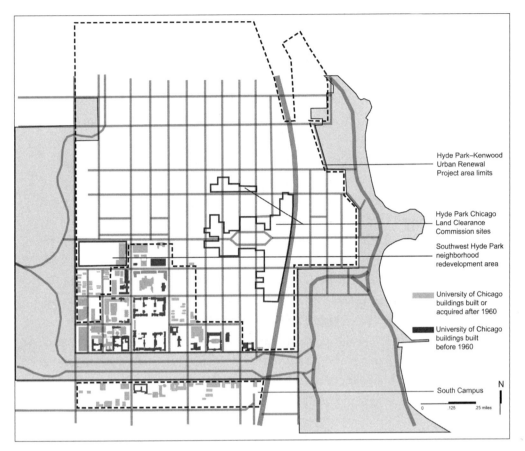

FIGURE 3.4 *The University of Chicago campus and landholdings in relationship to Hyde Park and Kenwood urban renewal in the mid-twentieth century.*

in any case where an educational institution is located in or near an urban renewal project area and the governing body of the locality determines that, in addition to the elimination of slums and blight from such area, the undertaking of an urban renewal project in such area will further promote the public welfare and the proper development of the community.[40]

When the *Chicago Sun-Times* reported on this change in April 1960, focusing on how it might assist the city in the purchase of land at the South-Side Railroad Terminal site for a new campus for the University of Illinois, it also reported that it would aid the University of Chicago in its expansion in Hyde Park. The article concluded, "A number of the nation's leading urban universities joined in asking Congress to pass the new section. They emphasized that if urban universities are to service and serve an increasing number of students a way has to be found for them to expand. Nearly all the universities are 'land locked.' Cities have grown up around them."[41]

The triangular set of relationships among the identification of processes of urban change (begun by Burgess, Robert E. Park, Lewis Wirth, and their colleagues), the study of contemporary urban change (continued by the Chicago Community Inventory under the auspices of Philip Hauser and Evelyn Kitegawa at the University of Chicago), and the University of Chicago's own involvement in urban renewal are highly complex; the space available here does not allow for their elaboration. And although the university's work in this area was not driven by its social scientists, they did not fight against it. Hauser commented, "Hyde Park Kenwood will become a pilot and model community for the entire nation, demonstrating that man not only can build a city, but can also prevent its decay."[42] Indeed, the university's influence in urban renewal would not have an impact only on the neighborhoods directly surrounding the campus; it would also influence citywide planning and policy decisions, ultimately leading to federal-level legislation that would provide mechanisms for university urban renewal projects nationwide.

The urban design and planning communities were well aware of the way urban renewal would affect urban campuses. An *Architectural Forum* article stated in 1963, "The urban university—once a city-within-a-city—is under growing pressure to expand its facilities. In this expansion, it is beginning to come face to face with unexpected problems—and unexpected opportunities."[43] It reported that more than sixty-four universities had availed themselves of various forms of urban renewal funding.[44] Enabled, as it often was, by uniting the needs of higher education with the needs of the city under the umbrella of urban renewal, midcentury campus design would also reflect the tenets of modern urbanism, well illustrated by campuses such as IIT. However, urban renewal and modernism met one another most thoroughly in the design of a public university, UICC, where location, demographics, mission, and form would come together in a process of negotiation leading to what would be called "a model for the modern urban university."[45]

4

Classrooms off the Expressway:
A New Mission for Higher Education

There have been many great projects constructed in Chicago . . . but none will mean so much to the people as the University of Illinois at Chicago Circle.

Richard J. Daley, *Chicago Daily News* supplement, 1965

T he new interstate expressways of the mid-twentieth century vastly changed the orientation of the nation's metropolitan regions, but they had an equally enormous impact on local geography. Chicago would be tethered to this system by a series of expressways, three of which intersect just to the west of the center of the city in the very location where the 1909 *Plan of Chicago* called for the building of a vast civic center. The then newly named Circle Interchange cuts the central area of the city into four quadrants, with the Loop, or downtown area, occupying the northeast quadrant. In the 1950s, much of the southeast quadrant, or the South Loop, was occupied by the vast railroad terminal network that Mayor Richard J. Daley hoped to consolidate to make way for a new University of Illinois campus and middle-class residential development. It was hoped that the northwest quadrant would absorb expanded development from the Loop. To the southwest, diagonally across the interchange, lay one of the oldest residential districts of the city, newly dubbed Harrison–Halsted, with Hull-House sitting at its northeast corner. Until the 1950s, this area—the Near West Side of Chicago—consisted of the industrial district located to the west of the South Branch of the Chicago River as it ran alongside the city's downtown, and the immigrant tenement district that ran west of these factories and warehouses. *Hull-House Maps and Papers* largely surveyed the portion of neighborhood that extended westward from the river to the Hull-House Settlement on Halsted Street, but the neighborhood continued to the west of the settlement for approximately another mile.[1] This neighborhood would become the location of the fierce contest between its residents and those who sought to locate the new University of Illinois campus adjacent to the new interchange.

Daley's image of the new Chicago he was working to build was supported by two mutually exclusive concepts: the importance of maintaining established neighborhoods and the need to modernize the city as a whole. Daley and the politicians, businessmen, and urban residents who supported him saw the renewal of the city as essential to its survival within the new urban region.[2] The University of Illinois at Chicago Circle (UICC) campus was an essential part of this vision, becoming to urban renewal what Hull-House had been to earlier urban reform. Although the replacement of the settlement and its surroundings by the new campus was, in the end, coincidental, retrospectively, the history of the neighborhood suggests a kind of inevitability. The future of the tenement district tied to the industries adjacent to the Chicago River would be called into question as manufacturing disappeared from the city, and the highways that replaced the river as connections to the growing region would further exacerbate the neighborhood's decline. As its residents were working to preserve and rebuild their community through the city's renewal processes, others were working toward identifying a site that could accommodate a new industry: mass higher education.

Locating the UICC Campus

Throughout the 1950s and early 1960s, and even through the period of campus construction, the calling defined for the new UICC was in constant flux and highly volatile. As late as 1972 the president of the University of Illinois stated, "No issue related to the mission of the University of Illinois and its basic planning assumptions has been so mired in uncertainty and controversy as the future of the Chicago Circle Campus."[3] The process of locating the campus and negotiating between the needs of the city and those of the university were simultaneous with the development of the new campus's academic programs, curricula, and mission. Its first chancellor, Norman Parker, at some point after the campus's opening, made the most concise statement, recognizing its specific *urban* mission: "From its inception, the new campus has functioned as an agency to study the problems of the urban society. The University is constantly being challenged by its urban location and by the unique role it can play in contributing to the quality of urban life."[4] Inherent in his statement is the notion that the way a university researches a city has an impact both on its physical relationship to that city and on future urban action. Until that point, the building of the campus was conceived instrumentally. As an appendage of the University of Illinois at Urbana–Champaign (UIUC), the original campus, known as the Chicago Undergraduate Division (CUD), was located on Chicago's Navy Pier adjacent to the mouth of the Chicago River (Figure 4.1). This undergraduate division satisfied an immediate postwar need: to offer a postsecondary education to returning war veterans whose "rehabilitation" was financed under the GI Bill of Rights. Established in June 1946, by the fall of that year CUD was offering a two-year course of study to more than 4,000 students.[5] By the early 1950s, the need to expand both the facilities and the curricula at the Navy Pier campus became apparent. Various committees and agencies began to conduct studies to determine what form a permanent solution might take and where it should be located.[6]

In 1953, E. L. Stouffer of the Physical Plant Department at CUD conveyed information to the University of Illinois regarding expansion plans at eight national and international urban campuses and recommended conducting an architectural competition for the design of a new campus once a site had

FIGURE 4.1 *Chicago's Navy Pier in use as the University of Illinois Chicago Undergraduate Division after World War II. Courtesy of Office of the UIC Historian.*

been selected. In April 1954, UIUC was asked to tabulate the number of students enrolled on its campus from various communities in and around Chicago in order to determine the need for expanded facilities directed toward the Chicago region.[7] The then president of the University of Illinois, Lloyd Morey, stated that the university would consider the location proposed by the Fort Dearborn project (a site north of the central branch of the Chicago River, planned by Mayor Martin Kennelly's administration), noting that the university would need to accommodate 88,000 students by 1970.[8]

In addition to potential conflicts with neighboring institutions of higher education that feared an expanded University of Illinois would negatively affect their enrollments, there was also considerable conflict within the University of Illinois itself. The planning of the campus and its curricula was marked by a constant tug-of-war between the faculty and administration of the flagship campus in Urbana–Champaign and their colleagues at CUD. By the late 1950s, two discrete proposals had been developed, one by the Navy Pier faculty and the other by committees in Urbana–Champaign. But as planning moved forward, Norman Parker, then a professor of mechanical engineering at UIUC and a member of the University of Illinois' planning committee, was named to coordinate the university's efforts in concert with Charles S. Havens, the head of the UIUC Physical Plant. UICC was to be a completely "new" institution, with little reference to the two-year program at Navy Pier from which it sprang, and was eventually to operate under its own administration and faculty rather than that of UIUC.

The decision as to where to locate the campus, however, created even greater conflicts, and it is the narrative of the process of determining its new home that reveals how embedded the new university became in urban renewal politics and how imbued it was with varying and often contradictory notions of what, specifically, an urban university needed to accomplish beyond providing more opportunities for higher education. Ultimately, the new campus would rise in "The Addams Area,"[9] the neighborhood directly to the west of Hull-House, but the decision to locate the UICC campus in the Near West Side was not a foregone conclusion when the university began to contemplate its new four-year campus. Although in retrospect the site makes considerable sense—it is directly accessible from the interchange that connects the then new major north–south and east–west highways, is directly accessible by bus and the L (the Chicago Transit Authority's elevated lines), and is just over a mile from the Loop and under a mile from the university's medical school (Figure 4.2)—it did not appear on the initial

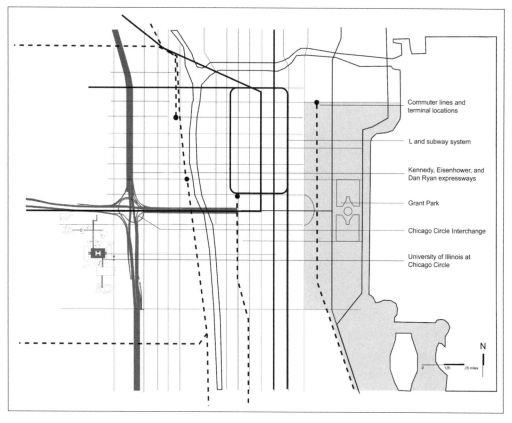

Commuter lines and
terminal locations

L and subway system

Kennedy, Eisenhower, and
Dan Ryan expressways

Grant Park

Chicago Circle Interchange

University of Illinois at
Chicago Circle

N

0   125   .25 miles

FIGURE 4.2 *Location of the University of Illinois at Chicago Circle campus in relationship to downtown Chicago, mass transit, and the interstate highway system in the early 1960s.*

list of approximately seventy sites considered by the Real Estate Research Corporation (RERC) and the project's architects, Skidmore, Owings & Merrill (SOM).[10]

Key to the RERC's study is that the university trustees did not see the city of Chicago itself as the obvious choice of location, preferring a suburban site that would most closely approximate the physical context of UIUC, an early land-grant university situated on a large expanse of land in a largely agricultural region.[11] One of the reasons for the difficulty in identifying a suitable site had to do with assumptions regarding scale and form. The university's board of trustees imagined the Chicago campus as a replica of the Urbana–Champaign campus, at least in form even if not in program, understanding a "campus" as a distinct sprawling precinct. Early studies advocated for a "low-rise" over a "high-rise" campus, and as a consequence, the trustees were looking for a site of at least 140 acres.[12] For this reason, the ideal site for the "urban" campus was a suburban location where the appropriate quantity of land was available and affordable, the population was middle-class, and the negative influences of urban life could be mitigated.[13] Four sites were seriously considered in the end: the Riverside golf course (suburban), Garfield Park (part of the Chicago Park District [CPD]), Meigs Field (an artificial peninsula jutting into Lake Michigan that contained a small airfield), and an area owned by the railroads (the so-called Railroad Terminal site). Occasionally, a new piece of landfill in Lake Michigan was also considered. Significantly, the focus turned to the city sites when Mayor Daley offered to pay any additional land-acquisition costs associated with an urban site. Given the mayor's offer, Garfield Park became the trustees' first choice within the city limits, as the land was clear of buildings and distinctly nonurban in character.[14] However, as we have seen, Mayor Daley's first choice, as indicated in the city's 1958 renewal plans, was the Railroad Terminal site. Daley and the strong business interests represented in the Loop saw the campus as an important part of downtown revitalization programs, infrastructure development, and the desire to stem the loss of businesses to the suburbs.[15]

The complex decision process was driven by the urban dynamics of the time, as the location of the campus did not mean the same thing to all communities. Such a large educational institution and those who would inhabit it would affect different communities differently. For example, the residents of Riverside, a suburb at the western edge of the city, were overwhelmingly against acquiring the campus, fearing a disruption of their neighborhoods by the predictable influx of urban students and traffic. Garfield Park, located on the west side of the city, "open" by virtue of being a park, would have entailed a transfer of land from the CPD and court proceedings to change its use. However, unlike their suburban neighbors, many members of the communities west of Garfield Park were in favor of the campus because it was seen as a potential buffer between their neighborhoods and the influx of largely African American residents starting to move into the blocks east of the park. This community was willing to give up the park, which they deemed dangerous and unruly anyway, in exchange for the protection of their own blocks from decline associated with racial succession.[16] Although initially the selection criteria for the site of the new university centered on location and physical features, other concerns were to become the basis of the political conflict that ensued.

a vast network of interlinked transportation systems. How did this proposal come about?

Urban renewal was key to this result. As previously discussed, at the end of 1959, Section 112 of the Federal Housing Act (FHA) offered a singular opportunity to Daley, the university trustees, and their planners. The Harrison–Halsted site met all the criteria of accessibility but had previously been ignored because of the difficulty of acquiring individual parcels of land and, later, because it had become a Chicago Land Clearance Commission (CLCC) area and was thought to be unavailable. Suddenly, it could be brought to the table for consideration. Although the change in the FHA had been advocated by existing—private and public—urban universities looking to expand and control their physical environment, Section 112 did not appear to preclude the possibility of condemning and clearing land for a new institution, particularly one that was public. The Harrison–Halsted site, which the CLCC was in the process of acquiring, had been designated for clearance, and it met many of Daley's requirements for bringing the university into the orbit of the Central Area, a criterion that the Garfield Park site failed to meet, at a time when negotiations over the Railroad Terminal consolidation had stalled. George Rosen, who studied the sequence of events leading to the decision, stated that Ira Bach, the city's commissioner of planning, started researching the Harrison–Halsted site almost immediately, in December 1959, while publicly the university was expressing interest in the Garfield Park site.[23] The lack of transparency of the process was one of its biggest problems. Echoing Rosen, Barbara Ferman stated, "Daley's top planners were researching the Harrison–Halsted site and were under strict orders not to reveal anything to the public *or even to university officials.* By the time Daley announced that the Harrison–Halsted corridor was an alternative site it was, in fact, the only site" (emphasis added).[24]

Although later contested in court, Section 112 provided the mechanism by which the Harrison–Halsted site could both qualify for federal urban renewal funding *and* become the site for the new university. Although there was a highly complex network of stakeholders in the decision—residents of Garfield Park, the Near West Side, and Riverside Park; Loop businesses; the railroads; and the university—many of whom were not consulted in the decision-making process, the outcome was part of a larger, national discussion about the relationship among higher education, urban renewal, and new urban forms. Nonetheless, this national phenomenon played out in Chicago through highly local political proclivities: Mayor Daley's fight to build the University of Illinois *in* Chicago—not just in its vicinity—was directly related to the city's activities to stem blight, a highly racially, ethnically, and economically charged concern.[25]

The city did not officially offer the land to the university until September 1960, although articles began to appear in the local press in the spring of 1960. At an April 28, 1960, meeting of the Hull-House board of trustees, James C. Downs, its president, who was also involved in the campus location negotiations through both the RERC and his role in the city, "called to the attention of the board a newspaper article stating that the Hull-House Land Clearance Area and some adjacent land might be offered to the University of Illinois as the Chicago site for the University in an attempt to reach a compromise between the Garfield Park location and the railroad site."[26] By June 1960, there was already a conversation between the city and the university comparing Garfield Park and Harrison–Halsted. The university stated its position as follows:

> The Harrison–Halsted project area is bounded on the south and west by blight and renewal areas, large areas of public housing and mixed commercial and industrial uses, which are poor environmental conditions. The Garfield Park Site, while surrounded on three sides by areas ready for renewal or conservation, appears to us to offer a better opportunity to establish a University environment. It should be noted that there are large commitments for public housing in the areas south and southwest of the Harrison–Halsted project.[27]

As the conversation proceeded, however, methods for isolating the campus from its context, including enlarging the site, committing to the nearby conservation area, and establishing systems to avoid having to relocate large infrastructure elements, made the site more palatable.[28] In July 1960, there was more definitive discussion in the press:

> Two prime criteria set for the selection of a site—immediate availability and accessibility for students—point to 55 acres in the corner formed by the intersection of the Congress and South Expressways. It is known as the Harrison–Halsted site, once one of the most deteriorated areas in the city. It has been taken over by the Chicago Land Clearance Commission.

At the same time, the NWSPB was working on a plan to stabilize the community through a combination of improved city services, small-scale local projects, and larger-scale renewal under the auspices of the Illinois Blighted Areas Redevelopment Act of 1947 and the FHA of 1949, which ultimately resulted in the land clearance and conservation sites previously discussed. The NWSPB saw urban renewal as a tool for stabilizing the Near West Side's declining neighborhoods. Fighting its own alderman and others on this issue, it actively engaged planners, architects, and developers to reenvision its neighborhood.[44] Several community leaders who first worked with the NWSPB to garner the appropriate designation and funding for renewal projects would later find themselves in a quandary when their priority—new housing—gave way to the state and city's priority, a new University of Illinois campus.

Florence Scala, who would later become the outspoken leader of the community groups that fought the university's and city's eventual desire to locate the new University of Illinois campus in the Harrison–Halsted redevelopment area, was the token woman—"our housewife"—on the NWSPB and a keen observer of demographic, physical, and political shifts in the neighborhood from the end of World War II through the beginning of the twenty-first century.[45] Scala stated that there were people eager to move out of the area and that the neighborhood did fit the official designation of an "area of slums and blight," but she also insisted that it was not a slum. Her description of the plans for the new neighborhood suggests a superblock garden city of low-rise and high-rise buildings scattered around an urban green, devoid of the bane and danger of traffic (Figure 4.6).[46] The plans developed for the Harrison–Halsted neighborhood in the 1950s closely followed the tenets of midcentury urban planning, with its separation of vehicular and pedestrian traffic, large expanses of open green space, and lack of direct relationship between buildings and street frontage, not unlike the majority of large public housing projects built around Chicago at the time. Residents of the area began to receive letters from the CLCC notifying them of the intent to purchase their homes in the fall of 1959.[47] How many intended to return to the neighborhood after the new housing was built remains unclear.

However, by the mid-1950s, Hull-House was no longer working directly with the NWSPB; rather, it established the separately controlled Hull-House Citizen's Participation Project (HHCPP) to assist its neighbors to prepare for urban renewal through neighborhood canvassing and information meetings.[48] The urban renewal included the possibility that cooperative housing

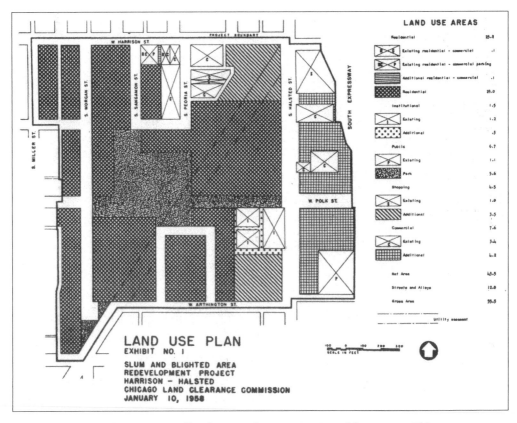

FIGURE 4.6 *Designation of land uses and reorganization of the street grid into a superblock of residential space organized around a central park for the Harrison–Halsted redevelopment area in 1958 and the location of the anticipated expressways. Much of this Chicago Land Clearance Commission site would become the University of Illinois at Chicago Circle campus. Hull-House sits at the eastern edge of this area. Chicago Land Clearance Commission.*

would be part of new residential development.[49] As others have noted, by this time the process was rife with conflicts of interest. In the early spring of 1960, trustees were discussing an extensive capital campaign to upgrade, remodel, and secure the structure of the buildings of the settlement.[50]

The End of the Hull-House Campus

In a "personal note" to Norman Parker, then vice president of UICC and later its chancellor, Florence Scala addressed a town–gown relationship made extreme by urban conditions:

What I really want to say is that I am *truly sorry* that we are in conflict. I have no stomach for battles with anyone, particularly with people like yourself who have devoted a lifetime to education. Unfortunately, we in the Near West Side are in the position of opposing the University *and* the city government. It is unavoidable. Naturally, our real quarrel is with the Mayor [Richard J. Daley] and his advisers, but he keeps aloof from it all and pretends not to notice us. We are forced to attack in another way and so we must challenge your plans. This must go on until one of us is removed from the scene.[51]

Scala had become the leader of the Harrison–Halsted Community Group (HHCG), which protested against the campus when the university accepted the Harrison–Halsted site in February 1961. The battle only came to an official end in May 1963 when the U.S. Supreme Court rejected an appeal to declare the government actions illegal. The HHCG organized marches in the neighborhood and the Loop, met with the mayor, held sit-ins in the mayor's office and protests outside his home, attempted to attract the attention of national leaders, and ultimately raised funds and organized to mount a legal battle. The group consisted of Italian, Mexican, African American, and Greek residents,[52] but the Italian women were out in front and the fight was closely identified with the person of Scala. Indeed, the interethnic and to some degree interracial dimension of the HHCG is in direct contrast to the HHCPP's image of tensions within the community, probably because one thing all residents agreed on was that they did not want their community displaced by the campus. The press portrayed their battle as one of neighborhood-bound tradition versus progress, and images of the women's protests (Figure 4.7) were often contrasted with images of the campus's future students. Images of the campus suggested it would be a harbinger of urban transformation.

The media played an important role in this conflict, though not in the final outcome.[53] For the debate was fought as much in and for the press as in the spaces of the city. The battle was seen as one of a new university versus dilapidated homes, students versus women and Mexicans (standing for the "ethnics" of the neighborhood), the city versus the neighborhood, rationality versus emotion, and the future versus the past. As the feminist author Iris Marion Young pointed out, these terms are typically seen in opposition and given a hierarchical reading: "The first term designates the positive unity on the inside, the second, less-valued term designates the leftover outside."[54]

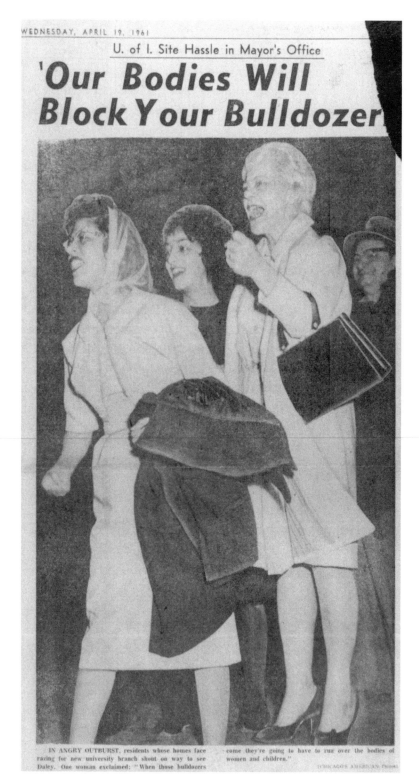

U. of I. Site Hassle in Mayor's Office

'Our Bodies Will Block Your Bulldozer'

IN ANGRY OUTBURST, residents whose homes face razing for new university branch shout on way to see Daley. One woman exclaimed: "When those bulldozers come they're going to have to run over the bodies of women and children."

CHICAGO'S AMERICAN Photo

FIGURE 4.7 *Harrison–Halsted community women protesting against the decision to place the University of Illinois campus in their neighborhood.* Chicago's American *photograph, April 19, 1961; courtesy of* Chicago Tribune. *All rights reserved; reprinted with permission.*

The women—"Our Bodies Will Block Your Bulldozers"[55]—brought "emotion," "desire," and "affinity," previously understood as private, into the public realm, threatening its unity and reason. Scala attached documentation in her letter to Parker carefully deconstructing the root of the problem: an urban site within a dense city and a nonurban organizational model were mutually exclusive. She and her advisers suggested that for an urban campus, the university should consider urban architectural forms: a dense collection of mid- and high-rise buildings, better suited to integration with the space of the city and easier to site.[56]

Two Chicago commentators of the time, Jack Mabley and John Madigan, illustrate the various ways in which the conflict was narrated. Mabley responded to the trustees' decision to accept the Hull-House site with a column titled "U of I—Off Pier into the Slums" and continued to support the local community in what he saw as a "David and Goliath" fight.[57] Mabley saw the issue as not slums but self-determination: "These men and women are fighting for their homes. It is an intensely personal thing with them. They believe they are right and I have not yet heard one person say they are not."[58] Mabley's own newspaper did not agree: "There are times when [people] are forced to move despite their wishes, either for their own good, or for the good of the community."[59] John Madigan of WBBM-TV Chicago, however, gave specific names to the combatants—Florence Scala and Richard J. Daley. In several *Standpoint* programs broadcast during 1961, Madigan urged Scala to back down:

> We sympathize with those residents of the area who don't want to be uprooted. We agree this is not a slum. We've seen evidence of the care most of the residents have given this aging community. We're aware that the first urban renewal plan for the vicinity was chiefly residential. . . . But WBBM-TV agrees with the Mayor that the Mrs. Scalas should try and balance this hardship against the *bright future ahead*. [Emphasis added][60]

Madigan appeared to be particularly discomfited by the lack of docility of the "Mrs. Scalas" who had "threatened" to bring their fight to the courts and had then followed through, leaving a "new sword, hanging over the Land Clearance Commission."[61] He took particular offense to Scala's remark "Tell Mr. Daley I surrender. He wins," after her home was bombed in the fall of 1962, stating that the "intemperate" and "inflammatory" nature of the protest was to blame. "We can't help wondering whether this act of terror could not have been avoided if the battle over the site had been conducted with less heat."[62] Despite the relative civility of their events, the protesters were, in the end, defending their homes.[63] As the group became savvier, media coverage increased. While the city was pursuing condemnation suits, the community organization had hired lawyers and was suing the city in state and federal court. In response to a sit-in in his office, Daley angrily responded to the neighborhood activists: "You're not going to stop that university!"[64]

In November 1962, the U.S. Court of Appeals for the Seventh Circuit dismissed the community's complaint, stating:

> The use to which plaintiffs desired the land to be put is undeniably a lawful public use. But, using the area acquired as a site for the Chicago branch of the University of Illinois is likewise a lawful public use. Courts have consistently denied the standing of citizens to challenge the choice made by public authorities between different and competing public uses. The legislature, through its lawfully created agencies, rather than "interested" citizens, is the guardian of the public needs to be served by social legislation.[65]

When the Supreme Court refused to review the case in May 1963, the protests ended, and the university awarded contracts for construction. As aggressive clearance got underway in early 1963, the *Chicago Daily News* ran a series of short interviews with "Hold Out" residents under the title "A Tragedy Called Progress Stalks UI Site."[66] Classes were first held on the new campus in February 1965.[67]

In these battles, we see two clearly articulated and opposing images of a city undergoing rapid change. Residents, led by Florence Scala, were fighting for their local neighborhood, which had been built on face-to-face communication, church connections, and family-run businesses. However, often forgotten in discussions of this period is the fact that those protesting the campus were protesting not urban renewal itself but, rather, the substitution of the university for the new residential district they had been hoping would preserve their community, as they were in agreement as to its dilapidated physical condition. Indeed, their own children would be beneficiaries of the new urban campus. On the other end of the spectrum were business leaders clearly banking on the city's overall "renewal"—bankers, automobile showroom dealers, and hotel owners—who were less concerned with who or what inhabited the site. These groups were eager to join the larger regional city. A WBBM *Special Paper* broadcast at the time of the opening of the campus documents the important role the site played in the history of Chicago; the loss of the community is only briefly mourned as a necessary consequence of a heroic new city of urban expansion and renewal, embodied by the campus and its students and faculty.

Within this context, the Hull-House complex (Figure 4.8) could only be seen as a throwback to the nineteenth-century city, its architectural style, interior spaces, and engagement with the life of the street irrelevant in a city of superblocks and modern architecture. Although many staff members and residents at Hull-House sided with the HHCG, the Hull-House Association pursued its plans to move its headquarters and decentralize its activities, selling the buildings and land to the university for $875,000. William F. Deknatel, an architect and president of the association, wrote to "Friends of Hull House" in May 1961, "Since Hull House is a service institution, not bricks and mortar, we are looking to our future in another area of great need, where we will carry forward our program of service to people." But he urged in his press release and in testimony on behalf of the board of trustees to the Housing and Planning Committee of the Chicago City Council that the buildings remain intact and be used in some way associated with the objectives of the work of Jane Addams.[68] Letters in support of the retention of the settlement buildings came from architects such as Ben Weese of the Chicago Heritage Committee and Earl H. Reed of the Committee on Preservation of Historic Building. Local citizens, including Scala, former Hull-House residents and current staff, and others, testified in front of the Chicago City Council and put forward additional letters from around the nation. In June, the university agreed to preserve a portion of the buildings. In the university's opinion, which reflected the ongoing work on the campus design, the buildings were not suitable for university use, and the "work of Jane Addams" could be accomplished "either through the retention, incorporation or relocation on-site of the *original* Hull House building or at least a portion thereof" (emphasis added).[69]

It was in this context that Illinois senator Paul Douglas issued a press release on July 10, 1961, scolding the university for its "projected vandalism":

> [Saving the original Hull mansion if it is rebuilt] is something, but it is not much. The University is being given 106 acres of land by the federal and local governments and hence by the citizenry. Thousands of good Americans are being turned into the streets to oblige the

FIGURE 4.8 *Hull-House Social Settlement elevation facing Halsted Street prior to demolition; view from land cleared in preparation for expressway construction (circa 1961). Jane Addams Memorial Collection (JAMC-0000-0134-1035), Special Collections, University of Illinois at Chicago Library.*

FIGURE 4.9 *Hull-House Social Settlement after demolition in an area cleared for the University of Illinois at Chicago Circle campus, showing the two buildings of the thirteen-building complex that were preserved. The building to the left, the Residents' Dining Hall, was moved and turned prior to construction of the campus; the third-story addition to the original Hull-House, on the right, was removed prior to remodeling. Courtesy of Jane Addams Memorial Collection (JAMC-0000-0315-0452), Special Collections, University of Illinois at Chicago Library.*

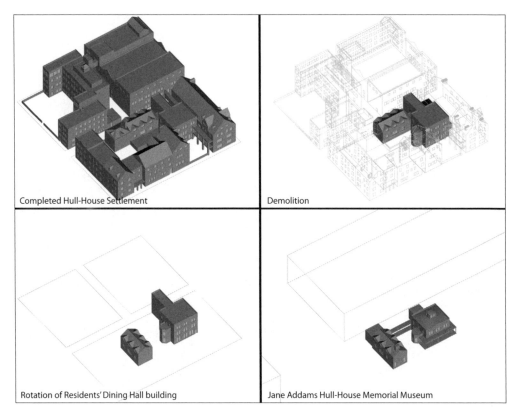

Completed Hull-House Settlement

Demolition

Rotation of Residents' Dining Hall building

Jane Addams Hull-House Memorial Museum

FIGURE 4.10 *Hull-House Social Settlement sequence of demolition and reconstruction.*

University. The University in turn should be willing to preserve a much larger share of the block at 800 S. Halsted Street, so that it may continue to be a tangible inspiration to the tens of thousands who will study there and to Americans of all ages.[70]

Whether in its present or modified condition, it is clear that the value of the complex was more as a symbol than as a functioning part of the city or an integrated part of the new campus, and the subsequent decision to demolish the majority of the complex and "restore" two of its buildings (Figures 4.9 and 4.10) reflected this view. There were some early attempts to retain some settlement-connected activities in the buildings that were to remain, but none of these came about.[71]

In 1963, with plans for the campus and its buildings awaiting implementation, there was little time for nuanced discussion of the integration of old and new pedagogical projects. The University of Illinois Foundation

FIGURE 4.11 *Demolition of the Hull-House Social Settlement, 1963. Courtesy of Jane Addams Memorial Collection (JAMC-0000-0371-0968), Special Collections, University of Illinois at Chicago Library.*

inaugurated a national campaign to raise private funds for a Hull-House restoration.[72] The buildings were closed in June, and on August 10, 1963, the *Chicago Daily News* carried an image of the only two buildings that remained with an arrow (inaccurately) showing how the Residents' Dining Hall was to be moved to "Shape [a] Historic Gateway for the New UI Campus."[73] As the new dean of the College of Architecture and the Arts, Leonard J. Currie, wrote to the Chicago Landmarks Commission, "The old house will stand out in all its architectural splendor, seemingly as though freshly emerged from its chrysalis. A symbol of tradition in a university dedicated to the future, Hull House may well be regarded as the soul of the new campus." The university was unsure how to treat the fragment that had become embedded in the complex; the decision was made to return the house "to approximately the state in which Miss Addams discovered it in 1889" to serve as a Jane Addams

Memorial.[74] Images of the destruction of the house (Figure 4.11), which oc-curred simultaneously with the building of the campus, revealed spaces and former activities that had long been forgotten, suggesting an urban history that the city contained but that was no longer seen: building fabrics and the lives of people hidden in the ruins left by neglect and time. In the nascent preservation movement of the 1960s, it was more important to preserve an object representing a period than a piece of the city that had been critical to its development. Hull-House was preserved and the UICC campus was built during a period uncomfortable with urban hybridity. Focused on the future of the city and its urban citizens, the modern campus replaced a conduit for neighborly pedagogy with a mechanism for efficient higher education for the masses.

FIGURE 5.2 *University of Illinois at Chicago Circle, circa 1970. Courtesy of the University of Illinois at Urbana–Champaign Archives, Photographic Subject File (Record Series 39/2/20), Box 98, Folder CHI 2-1 1967–74.*

him internalized the Burnham and Bennett concept of the civic center plaza as the "crossroads" of the city. Moving beyond the sensitivities of the battle over the site of just a year before, Buck referred to it as a "tract being cleared of slums and other buildings."[8] All journalistic, academic, and architectural coverage from this point forward replaced the grounded language of the neighborhood with the abstraction "slum-cleared land."[9]

A Sears, Roebuck and Company advertisement in a special supplement to the *Chicago Daily News* in September 1965 expresses the popular view of the campus most clearly (see Figure 5.3):

> In Chicago, the only thing growing faster than Sears is the University of Illinois. Congratulations on being at the center of things! . . . And we need you, the knowledgable [*sic*] person who can grow with us. Unlimited horizons. 27 Chicagoland Sears stores . . . more to come.[10]

The ad provides a striking visual summary of the argument for the campus and its unique position in the expanding territories of the Chicago region. Many other advertisements in the supplement, entitled "The University of Illinois Serves Chicago . . . Serves the State," echo the link between the baby-boom population and the needs of the city's industries. With a depiction of a ladder dramatically rising from the Chicago skyline, Illinois Central Railroad's ad declares, "For Mid-America's boys and girls: another ladder for climbing." Standard Oil saluted the campus, saying, "Caps off to the University of Illinois for its great cultural contribution to the Chicago scene . . . the new Circle Campus," as did Pepsi-Cola in an ad showing two students standing at the center of the campus with the new administration tower behind them; the ad reads, "A Chicago dream comes alive! Pepsi's proud."[11]

Students who arrived at the new campus fresh from their experiences on Navy Pier understood their role in this narrative. Arlene Norsym, a student at the time of the opening of the campus and now associate chancellor for UIC Alumni Relations, said of the move:

> Many of us came from Navy Pier, a wonderful but very straight-lined experience—great camaraderie—but now we were on a real campus. This was something that most of us were never going to have the opportunity to experience. We were as Richard J. Daley said, "his constituents," the children of the blue-collar families of Chicago who didn't have the funds to go away to school, but now we

FIGURE 5.3 *Sears, Roebuck and Company advertisement in the* Chicago Daily News *supplement celebrating the University of Illinois at Chicago Circle campus. "The University of Illinois Serves Chicago . . . Serves the State," special supplement,* Chicago Daily News, *September 25, 1965, 24.*

were on a real campus. I think the one word that we all said when we set foot here was "wow."[12]

Speaking of the buildings, she added, "These buildings were functional, they were durable, and they were like us, practical and edgy and ready to go to work and they did work, as long as they were maintained." The novelty of the campus, in particular the walkways and the forum, appears to have called forth attention and pride in step with the spirit of the times, with their newness a factor in the assessment.

The history of Hull-House and the presence of its remnants on the campus were not lost in this narrative. The role of the campus in fulfilling its progressive mission also appeared in the *Chicago Daily News* supplement in a full-page ad, placed by the Carson Pirie Scott and Company department store, that sounded a cautionary note. Using an image that highlights the renovated Hull-House in the foreground and shows the administration tower of the campus rising in the background, more than half the page is devoted to a quotation from *Twenty Years at Hull-House* that reads in part:

> I recall Miss Lathrop's Plato club and an audience who listened to a series of lectures by Dr. John Dewey on "Social Psychology," as genuine intellectual groups consisting largely of people from the immediate neighborhood, who are willing to make "that effort from which we all shrink, the effort of thought."

Challenging the university to live up to its commitment to Chicago, the ad closes, "We expect great things from the University of Illinois at Chicago Circle."[13]

Precedents for the Design of a New Urban Campus

The choice of planners and designers for UICC greatly influenced the results. SOM was involved with the project for the new campus early on. Founded in 1936, by the early 1960s, SOM had emerged as one of the largest and most powerful architectural firms in the United States, with four regional offices capable of providing clients with a full range of architectural, interior design, engineering, master planning, and construction management services. SOM's organization matched those of their corporate clients and the growing building industry: "To work, we must have volume. An efficient set of master builders can eat up a lot of work. Volume meant power. We would try to change men's minds."[14] SOM's reach—its geographical distribution around the continental United States, the range of design and engineering services it could provide, and the variety of its corporate, institutional, and governmental client base—was extensive. The firm's work included the two building types most desired by postindustrial corporate culture: downtown office towers and suburban office parks, sometimes called "corporate campuses." Netsch, chief architect of the UICC project, had attained fame and notoriety as SOM's young, willful designer of the U.S. Air Force Academy in Colorado in the late 1950s. He was known for his interest in experimenting with new building techniques, materials, and architectural programming. He also violated the vertical organization of the SOM office, preferring to work in a "studio" environment with a full team of designers, technicians, and site managers.[15]

Precedents for Netsch's thinking can be understood along two lines, the first urbanistic, the second architectural. Unlike many rising architects in Chicago at the time, who were educated by Mies van der Rohe at IIT, Netsch was educated at the Massachusetts Institute of Technology (MIT) in the late 1930s, just as its school of architecture was shifting from a Beaux-Arts to a modern emphasis in design. Speaking of early influences on his thinking, Netsch recalled Sigfried Giedeon's book *Space, Time, and Architecture* as the "school bible."[16] However, although interested in theories of modern architectural and urban development, Netsch was not a member of the Congrès internationaux d'architecture moderne (CIAM), an influential organization of architects and urbanists, whose modernist principles of urban planning arrived in the United States largely through the auspices of Harvard University, Giedeon, and Jose Luis Sert, a Catalan architect who became CIAM's postwar president.[17] Although Netsch was not directly connected to those circles of thought, UICC would come to model many significant CIAM principles.[18]

What made CIAM's approach different from earlier ideas about the city? Architectural historian Eric Mumford demonstrated the way the concept of designing a "functional city" advocated by CIAM members shifted away from nineteenth-century urban design principles toward "a more 'scientific' approach to urban planning, based on the collection and analysis of physical and social data," an approach that had already attained significant international recognition by the early 1930s. The Declaration of La Sarraz, the founding document of CIAM, written in 1928, states, "Urbanization cannot be conditioned by the pretensions of a pre-existent estheticism: its essence is of a functional order."[19] CIAM thinking would inform postwar American urbanism, which Mumford claimed "implemented some CIAM-like approaches in the service of a politically conservative urbanistic vision of remade American downtowns served by highways linked to commuter suburbs," different in tenor from the largely socially progressive ideas that underscored the European architects' and urbanists' writings and hypothetical projects between the wars.[20] The question of the creation or stabilization of communities within decentralizing urban development marked almost all planning and architectural design of this period, whether to repair bombed-out European cities, to define new spaces for democratic action in postcolonial nations, or to protect American commercial centers against suburbanization, and CIAM members believed that their approach could be used in each of these instances. In numerous examples around the world, however, the application of CIAM's approach worked as much to further the decentralization of cities, and often to displace their existing inhabitants, as to restore the importance of the central city in postwar urban geography.

The "CIAM grid" (1948) was developed as a classification tool that allowed comparison of different designs and plans. The grid breaks urbanism down into core functions: living, working, cultivating body and spirit, circulating, and miscellaneous.[21] Although there was not a direct correlation between the functions enumerated in the CIAM grid and the functions required for the university, the design process used in developing UICC mimicked that of CIAM designers, breaking down elements of the design into functional areas through a statistical analysis of needs, a segregation of functions based on that analysis, and a focus on circulation as the mechanism for uniting those functions. The UICC campus would come to share a number of features of CIAM-inspired urban design, in particular the separation and zoning of programmatic functions and the separation of circulation systems commonly seen in Le Corbusier's urban proposals, such as his Contemporary City for Three Million Inhabitants (1922). At the same time, it would move away from Miesian urbanism suggested by IIT.

From an architectural perspective, historian Robert Bruegmann cited Eero Saarinen's design for the General Motors Technical Center in Warren, Michigan (1947–1955), Gordon Bunshaft's design for the Connecticut General Life Insurance Company in Bloomfield, Connecticut (1954–1957), and the University of Mexico campus in Mexico City as influencing Netsch's design for the Air Force Academy.[22] They appear to be influential in the early schemes for UICC as well. The University of Mexico campus is illustrative for its ensemble of modernist building complexes placed around a large, open green and for the use of an arterial roadway system to isolate the campus from its surrounding context. The Connecticut General and General Motors buildings bear comparison for several reasons. They are among the most important examples of the transformation of the university campus into a generalized principle of spatial organization for a corporate culture resituated on large tracts of suburban land. Iconic images of the Connecticut General building show it sitting within a large expanse of agricultural landscape, emulating old images of rural college campuses. Bunshaft's complex for the American Can Company follows a similar organization, being situated in the more wooded topography of Greenwich, Connecticut (1970). Bunshaft's buildings organize large numbers of individuals in large horizontal buildings by insinuating courtyards within the depths of the large floor plans in order to disrupt the neutral structure and suggest a subtle hierarchy of office and circulation. It is the logic of the skyscraper as it finds its way back to the ground. By contrast, Saarinen's complex is more literal in its uses of the organizational principles of the American campus while twisting the nature of its iconography. Here the campus lawn became a large, rectangular pool of water, the library became a domed display room, and the clock or bell tower became a water tower. Most significantly, the scale requires the automobile for mobility.

But as the UICC design progressed, it began to depart from these models. First, as Netsch often noted, he had no desire to repeat the design of the Air Force Academy. Second, once a site was settled upon, he was able to begin to address the design as an "urban land" problem rather than as an architectural problem, by which he meant that the overall design of the campus in its urban context was more important than the design of the individual buildings.[23] Finally, he recognized that the education of cadets and coeds required different pedagogies and spaces. In the case of Air Force cadets, there was to be no individuation. From uniform to bunk to dining hall to classroom to drill, each element had to march in formation. This is part of the drama of the Air Force Academy. In the case of students, the diversity of urban life was part of the educational experience, and Netsch's idea was to help it find its way into the space of the campus.

Designing for the Urban Mission

To the University of Illinois board of trustees, the new campus was neither a problem of urban design nor directly connected to the problems of American cities. As we have seen, the issue at hand was where and how to accommodate Illinois' growing numbers of college students. As early as 1951, the state of Illinois directed the university to establish a permanent Chicago campus.[24] A 1954 technical report prepared by the university's Subcommittee on Physical Planning for the Chicago Undergraduate Division (CUD) shows a clear bias in favor of traditional campus forms, recommending that "the Chicago Undergraduate Campus of the University of Illinois be developed with low rise buildings except where functional requirements dictate otherwise." Although the report gives ample consideration to construction and land costs, there is an underlying concern about the relationship of education to environment and of student to faculty. "Human scale in building is an essential. . . . Students are not bees to be crowded into a hive. The educational process is intended to create an intellectual freedom which cannot be garnered from a reading or lecture factory." High-rise buildings would create a problem of flow that would be "exactly contrary to sound educational and functional planning" because they would tend "further to segregate students from faculty." The report also favors low-rise buildings because "the varied elements characterized in low rise buildings develop or give expression to individuality rather than anonymity, in contrast to the uniformity required by economic necessity in higher rise buildings."[25] This recognition of individuality versus anonymity and variety versus uniformity, suppressed in the early stages of physical planning for the project, reappeared when the final site was selected. Given the restrictions put in place by the university, the early designs suggest a sprawling urbanism that takes many of its cues from the new IIT campus. What distinguishes the final design of the campus from those earlier proposals is the embodiment of a large-scale image of the city within the master plan's overall form. UICC was not a piece of the new city; it *was* the new city. Although its design began as a response to both an urban and an educational need, it was resolved as a form of embedded pedagogy: in addition to utilizing modern pedagogical methods, it was designed to teach a lesson about modern American urban design.

The final form of the campus design was an intersection of pedagogy directed toward the commuting student, developed by Norman Parker, then a professor of mechanical engineering at the University of Illinois at Urbana–Champaign (UIUC); an architecture focusing on the movement of those students, developed by SOM; and oversight by the city of Chicago. The SOM team was headed up by Netsch as the design partner and included Fred W. Kraft as the administrative partner, Ralph Youngren as an assistant

community—particularly as regards the training of specialized personnel for a wide range of occupational fields.

4. To encourage the cultivation of the rich resources of the metropolitan area for cultural, social, economic, and scientific–technical education.[36]

An important aspect of this early report is its hint at a physical arrangement of the campus:

> There should be a central core of the campus consisting of liberal arts, the library, the teletorium lecture center, and the Union. Around the periphery of this core should be commerce, engineering, creative arts, physical and biological sciences structures, and the administration building. Further out on the periphery should be the facilities for physical education, military science, and the physical plant. Sufficient space for expansion should be allowed in each general area.[37]

In addition, the recommendations ask for a number of functional locations or relationships, among them: that there be "one central library," that "humanities should be centrally located," that there be "a teletorium or lecture center," and that the administration building be located at the "front door" of the campus. Finally, the report states, "Classrooms should be interchangeable for maximum use."[38] This description comes very close to the conceptual plan of the campus, what Netsch described as the "drop of water" scheme, a campus organized in a series of rings of activity radiating out from a dense center of shared teaching facilities.[39] The "drop of water" proposal on which the final design was based was for Netsch "the breakthrough idea for an urban campus. It was brought up as this being the scheme for a new university . . . the center of learning pushing out to the separate disciplines."[40] In late 1960, mission and design began to coalesce.

It is difficult to construct a linear sequence of events leading to the ultimate form of the UICC campus from the planning documents, but it is clear that between the university's acceptance of the site in February 1961 and the presentation of conceptual diagrams and a model to the public in September of the same year, the campus design was fully fleshed out. Unlike the city's proposal for the campus, which located high-rise buildings adjacent to the highways and relocated major arteries such as Halsted Street, SOM's early schemes were more restrained, locating the majority of academic buildings between Harrison and Taylor streets at the north and south and Halsted and Morgan streets at the east and west. In these schemes (Figure 5.4), large parking lots are located along Harrison Street at the west and below Taylor Street on the south, parcels that could be used for later campus expansion. Playing fields sit on the awkward parcels between the campus and the new expressways. Most notably, at this point the issue of residential development was resolved: there was to be none, which reflected the differing priorities of the university and the city. The design consists of three major building types: small-footprint slab high-rises, large-footprint courtyard buildings, and clusters of small classroom buildings. All are located so as to avoid major infrastructure elements and are arrayed around a large open space at the center. The four large courtyard buildings terminate major north–south and east–west axes at the center of the campus; the high-rise buildings, arranged in a pinwheel configuration, complete the corners of the square. Smaller classroom clusters sit within the center of this space, connected to one another through a smaller network of paths. By May 1961, the focus on intellectual and physical communication became more extreme, as a large podium-like building takes its place at the center of the campus, establishing a clear focus for the design.

The large space at the center of the campus was significant because it suggested a university program organized around shared facilities rather than shared academic concerns and served to bring together several design criteria: the application of new technologies, a flexible and varied environment, ease of access by car and rapid transit, interdisciplinary interaction, and incremental growth. The common functional thread running through all these themes was the need to move large numbers of students on and off campus and to their classes in a timely fashion. Shared facilities would compel the desired interdisciplinary contact, as students and faculty would cross paths as they moved into and out of the central lecture centers. Thus, the academic community would be formed through functional requirements rather than through specific departmental affinities. This solution was both utilitarian and deontological: it identified the most efficient means to achieve the greatest "good" and located a universal solution through impartial reason.[41]

Presentation sketches from May 1961 elaborate this proposal, which was to be built in two phases (Figure 5.5). In the second-phase version, the Lecture Center sits at the center of the site, with the library to its west and the

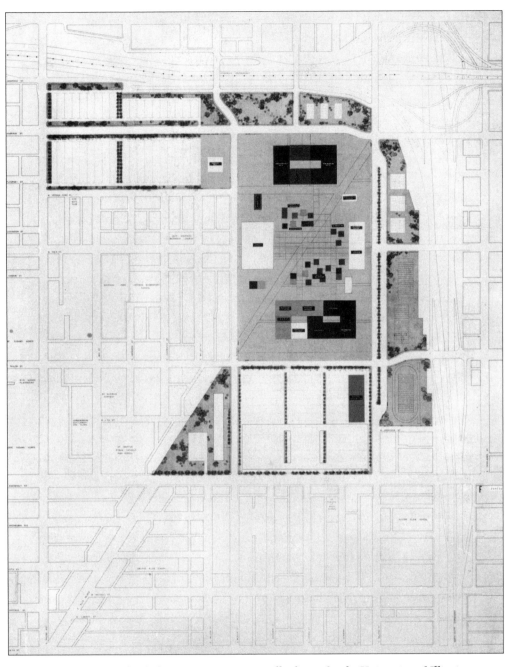

FIGURE 5.4 *Early Skidmore, Owings & Merrill scheme for the University of Illinois at Chicago Circle campus on the Harrison–Halsted site illustrating the general organization of the site. Courtesy of Skidmore, Owings & Merrill LLP.*

student center to its east. Smaller groupings of classroom buildings complement the Lecture Center and two large buildings—one housing the College of Fine Arts and Architecture and the other the College of Engineering—sit at the north and south boundaries. Of the four towers Netsch and his team originally proposed, three remain in the final design despite the university's request that there be none, although there are few teaching spaces in these buildings. The tallest, University Hall, contains the offices for the College of Liberal Arts and Sciences, the offices of the humanities faculty, and the offices and functions of the upper administration. This twenty-eight-story building locates the campus within the skyline of the city. The shortest tower sits next to the Chicago Circle Center, the student union, and contains offices devoted to student clubs and organizations. In the drawing, the final tower is labeled "faculty services," but it eventually became the offices of the math and physical science faculties. Later, a separate building was built to contain the offices for the social and behavioral sciences faculty, the College of Business, and the College of Urban Planning and Public Affairs on a site west of University Hall. In some iterations, an auditorium appears in this location. The major pedestrian circulation elements, the walkways, located one story above ground, are clearly evident in these sketches. They serve several functions: to bring students and faculty to the center of the campus from parking lots to the south and the L to the north, to link the smaller classroom buildings to the larger lecture centers, and, as they converge at the center, to form a large communal public space on top of the lecture centers. The axial walkways, Lecture Center, and high-rise buildings act in concert to connect the complex to the large scale of the city. Later, Dixon would refer to these elements as "the walkways," "the hub," and "the tower."[42] Often ignored in these discussions were the smaller classroom buildings that are grouped in more casual relationships on the ground.

Using this master plan, Steve Dawson of the landscape architecture firm Sasaki, Walker & Associates began to work on a landscape-development study. The Sasaki firm's reputation had been built on its work developing new landscapes resulting from postwar urban decentralization. In addition to its work with SOM on a number of suburban corporate campus projects, the firm was also responsible for the design of numerous new university campuses throughout the 1950s and 1960s. The Sasaki firm was most involved during the early stages of the landscape design for the UICC campus; early drawings show its design for the ground plane that was later modified by SOM.[43] A large-scale drawing (May 18, 1961) proposes further development

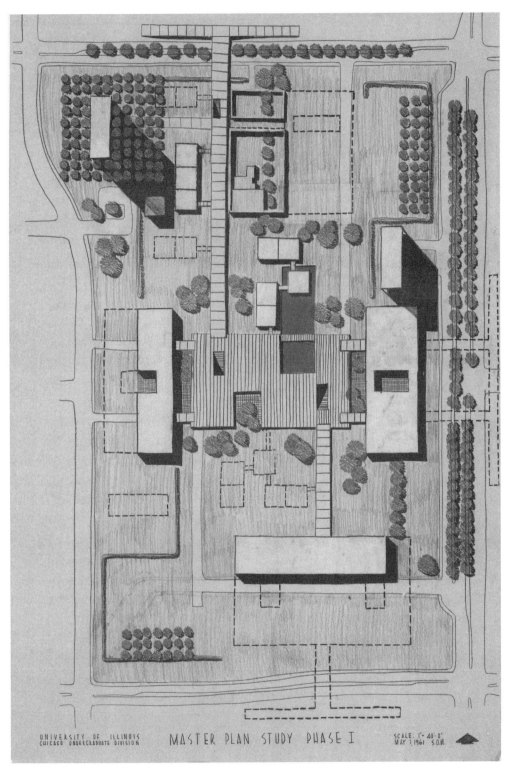

UNIVERSITY OF ILLINOIS
CHICAGO UNDERGRADUATE DIVISION   MASTER PLAN STUDY PHASE I   SCALE: 1"=40'-0"
MAY 1, 1961 S.O.M.

FIGURE 5.5 *University of Illinois at Chicago Circle May 1961 plan for the first of two construction phases, showing early development of the Forum/Lecture Center and walkways. Courtesy of Skidmore, Owings & Merrill LLP.*

of the ground plane to act as a foil to the urbanistic gestures of the raised infrastructure and buildings (Figure 5.6). The plan suggests a heavily forested, grassy ground plane and a loose system of paths defined by subtle changes in section. Here the campus is distinguished from its city surroundings by groves and hedges at interfaces with streets. Small entrances to the campus are cut into the hedges so that, unlike IIT's campus, the UICC campus would not be continuously open to the street grid. The buildings of the campus sit in a parklike setting and reach out to the city with walkways, gracing the skyline with towers. This was a new urban form, a new way to relate buildings and grounds to the city and a new way to bring that relationship about. Netsch and Dawson did not design a skyscraper or corporate campus, typical of the work of their offices at that time; they designed a model of the city as it was forming, a city with a new kind of central gathering space.

Work on the design of the campus proceeded through the summer (Figure 5.7), leading to a public unveiling of the scheme in September 1961. The architects' work focused the conceptual underpinning of the project, developed the architecture of the Lecture Center, and clarified the spatial experiences for the campus users. This work was presented through a model and a series of conceptual diagrams (Figure 5.8), addressing four themes: new teaching techniques, flexibility, variety in educational environment, and interdisciplinary opportunities. Using the RERC studies of the student population, surveys of the Navy Pier campus faculty to determine their teaching requirements, and projections of the number of students expected to enroll in each subject area, SOM developed images that digested and visually bridged the mass of statistical information, deploying it in diagrammatic expressions of physical space. The drawing for new teaching techniques—an electric-circuit diagram—suggests the way information would be circulated throughout the campus through audio and visual technologies, including television. Flexibility and variety are illustrated by a plan and a section showing the intermixing of disciplines throughout the buildings, particularly in the Lecture Center (as the "teletorium" would come to be known). The diagram of interdisciplinary opportunity highlights spaces of movement and interaction between people and information: the walkways and the forum, the library and the student center. These drawings are a map of relationships in which bodies, conceived as statistical abstractions, move unimpeded by hierarchical or disciplinary structures. In them, pedagogical planning and urban planning begin to mirror one another in the verbal, visual, and architectural language of postwar technological advancement.[44]

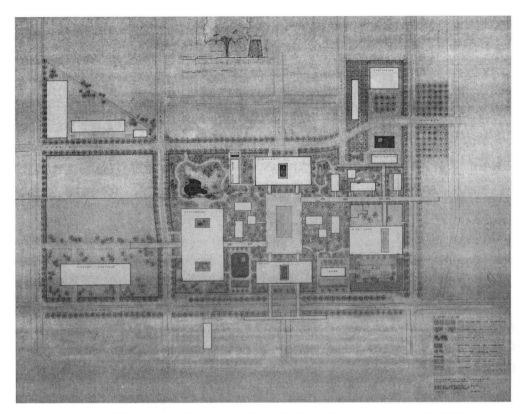

FIGURE 5.6 *University of Illinois at Chicago Circle landscape plan by Sasaki, Walker & Associates (May 18, 1961). The plan illustrates the contrast between the orthogonal organization of spaces associated with the buildings and walkway infrastructure and the fluid landscape of the remaining ground plane. The drawing also shows a detail for the proposed hedge around the campus. Courtesy of Skidmore, Owings & Merrill LLP.*

Midcentury Campus

Like other aspects of mid-twentieth-century urban planning, the architectural discourse on campus planning stressed the need for "functionalism," "interdisciplinarity," and "flexibility" to meet the growing and changing needs of higher education. In 1958, the Ford Foundation established the Educational Facilities Laboratories (EFL), a nonprofit organization that through the 1960s and 1970s studied the role of new technologies in the design of both buildings (or more largely, "facilities") and pedagogy, often with a specifically urban focus connected to urban renewal. As one report produced by EFL, *Bricks and Mortarboards: A Report on College Planning and Building,* from the early 1960s, states:

The problem is a more complex one than sheer numbers and building capacity. The decision-maker has another concern: new procedures and new technology are reshaping the academic process. The space built today for higher education must be adaptable to these new changes, and, therefore useful for many years to come.[45]

Although entirely novel in its design, the UICC campus was central to these discussions.[46] *Bricks and Mortarboards* cites the campus for its approach to interdisciplinarity:

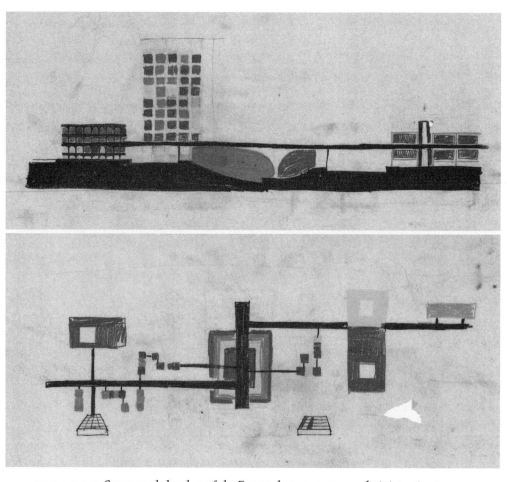

FIGURE 5.7 *Conceptual sketches of the Forum, lecture centers, administration tower (now University Hall), and the interconnecting walkway system. In the original, color coding indicated the disciplinary and interdisciplinary uses of each building. Skidmore, Owings & Merrill LLP.*

FIGURE 5.11 *Dr. Andrew Schiller lecturing (in absentia) in Rhetoric 101 in a classroom equipped for closed-circuit television. Courtesy of the University of Illinois at Urbana–Champaign Archives, Photographic Subject File (Record Series 39/2/20), Box 98, Folder CHI 2-1 Lecture Center.*

opening of the Chicago Circle campus—"All New Pioneering 'U'"—Thomas Buck referred to plans "to make the fullest use of the Chicago area as an 'educational resource'" through field trips and the hiring of business and industrial professionals as part-time teachers. The latter would have no need to actually come to the university, noted the dean of the College of Business: "Instead of personal appearances of men in business and industry, we plan to exploit the TV interview or press conference format developed in news and public affairs programs" (Figure 5.12).[58] Such programming was to be made possible by OIR, which would provide "the latest techniques in teaching—television, film, overhead projectors, automated laboratories, programmed instructions, teaching machines, and other new devices."[59] The relationship of the campus to the city, therefore, was mediated not by walls and gates but by new technologies and media. Nor did the campus dissolve into the city; campus and city were attached via transportation and media technologies that brought the advantages of the city into the center of the campus. All these maneuvers can be attributed to the goal of fulfilling needs: the need to accommodate a large number of students quickly, the need to move those students around the campus efficiently, and the need to teach them with a limited number of faculty. These concerns, as we have seen, were particularly relevant to Netsch, who brought them to bear on the campus's final form.

As initially built, the major campus features—the Forum, the walkway system, and University Hall—were clearly evident at a larger urban scale; like the expressway system itself, they were best understood from a helicopter. But on the ground, an entirely different scale was at work based on a stripped-down version of the original landscape plan. Three-story buildings clustered around small open courtyards where students could mingle at the thresholds of the buildings. These were not spaces built to accommodate 5,000 to 20,000 commuting students on fifty-minute lecture schedules; rather, they were intended for those slated for smaller classes and seminars. The contrast between these more intimate spaces—more loosely landscaped and programmed—and the larger scale of the great plaza was considerable. The landscape on the ground and on the walkways created opposing experiences and views (Figure 5.13). Netsch considered the design of the UICC campus as a "transitional" space, struggling between the complexity of the scale of the city and the scale of architecture.[60] Much more than the Air Force Academy, "where you have 2600 cadets marching en masse here and there" in highly regimented formation, the Chicago Circle campus was an attempt to address individuation within a mass environment.[61] The design wrestled

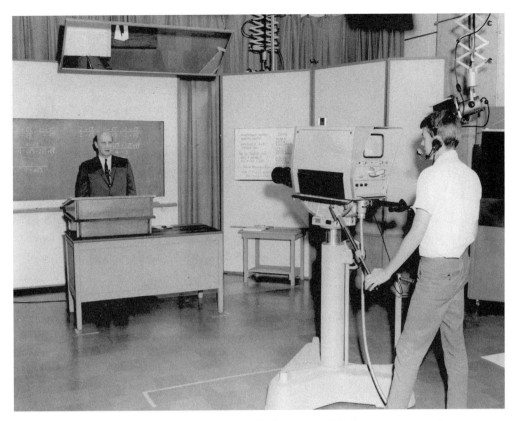

FIGURE 5.12 *Professor Kenneth H. Murphy lecturing in Mathematics 104 and 105. Courtesy of the University of Illinois at Urbana–Champaign Archives, Photographic Subject File (Record Series 39/2/20), Box 98, Folder CHI 2-1 Lecture Center.*

with the sticky problems of societal and educational groups coming to terms with large-scale institutions and of architectural, urban, and cultural communities uniting technological innovation and formal experimentation.

But it was the roofscape created by the elevated walkway system and Lecture Center that best expressed how the campus reflected Netsch's vision for a new urban landscape. In this sense, it was of a kind with numerous campuses around the country being rushed into production for swelling student enrollment.[62] As architectural theorist Oscar Newman noted in an *Architectural Forum* article on new campus design in the 1960s:

> It is not reading too much into the plans . . . to suggest that their designers are using them as instruments to express their aspirations and faith in high density urban environments. . . . Best of all,

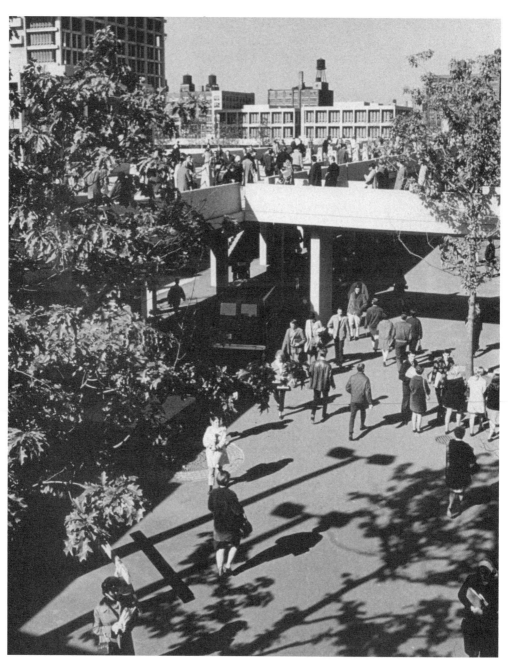

FIGURE 5.13 *Upper walkways and street-level ground plane in use during the early years of the campus. Courtesy of Orlando Cabanban/Office of the UIC Historian.*

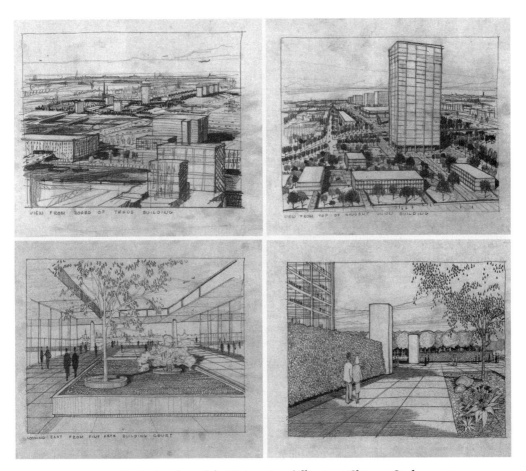

FIGURE 5.14 *Early sketches of the University of Illinois at Chicago Circle campus before final architectural design of the buildings. Upper images illustrate the campus's relationship to the city, lower images the spaces of the campus. Note the hedge separating the campus from the surrounding community in the lower right image. Courtesy of Skidmore, Owings & Merrill LLP.*

campus design stands out as a problem uniquely reflective of our time—a distillation of the needs and values we like to think of as being synonymous with our great, open, mobile, and progressive society. Universities are not just the most sophisticated of all our institutions, they may be, today, the most relevant.[63]

Like the other new campuses, UICC was its own high-density urban environment, but it was also situated within the city. As the first dean of the College of Architecture and the Arts marveled:

FIGURE 5.15 *Night view of the Forum and upper walkways illustrating the campus's position in the urban context. Courtesy of Orlando Cabanban/Office of the UIC Historian.*

> You can get on the subway in front of the SOM office at the Inland Steel Building downtown and in four minutes you can get off at the university station, go up the escalator, get on the pedestrian ramp, and go anyplace on this campus and never cross vehicular traffic. To do this in a city the size of Chicago is an entirely different thing than we have ever done before.[64]

The quotation exemplifies the great ambiguity of Netsch's campus: created by infrastructure and framed by buildings, it was of the city, not of the ground. As it reached out to the city, it simultaneously ignored its context, replicating the isolating tendencies of cloistered campuses such as the University of Chicago while rejecting their architectonic and spatial precedents. This is clearly seen in a series of small but highly detailed perspective sketches contained in the SOM's archives (Figure 5.14). Offering views to the campus from the Loop and to the city from the campus, they show the campus as part of the expanding city, linked to its skyline at the lake and expanding out to the suburbs to the north, south, and west. And whether or not Mayor Daley saw these sketches when he reviewed the project during the summer of 1961, they conform to the image of the city he was promoting on a larger scale. They would have confirmed his belief in the purpose and location of the new campus. Early aerial images of the campus at night illustrate its primary elements silhouetted against the sky, walkways extending to the horizon, and the Forum marking its center (Figure 5.15). The scene mirrors Chicago's own midcentury nighttime image: skyscraper, grid, and highways coming together at the new interchange.

6

Campus Revolt: The Reform of the Commuter University

The campus used to be called the University of Illinois at Chicago Circle. Perhaps the bureaucrats who named the University after a traffic circle got the campus they deserved.

Robert A. M. Stern, *Pride of Place*, 1986

Mayor Richard J. Daley considered the building of the campus at Chicago Circle to be one of his greatest accomplishments as mayor, on a par with the new expressways and public housing, modern, monumental answers to urban decay.[1] Speaking at a luncheon to celebrate the campus in October 1965, he hailed the University of Illinois at Chicago Circle (UICC) as "the first university to be created out of slum and blight."[2] Even as it was being built, however, the educational and urbanistic principles on which it was founded were coming under attack. Nationwide, students were protesting, not just against the Vietnam War, but also against the university as an institution embedded in larger urban, national, and global systems of power. Some of these protests went to the heart of the university's relationship to the surrounding city. As we have already seen, Jane Jacobs lambasted urban renewal as it was being practiced in Hyde Park–Kenwood around the University of Chicago. High-modern architecture as practiced by architects such as Ludwig Mies van der Rohe and deployed urbanistically at the Illinois Institute of Technology (IIT) was falling out of favor. Criticism of UICC was particularly vehement. Both because the campus design project was an extension of postwar American urbanization and because it was based in many ways on the physical forms and formulas that had shaped the postwar American city, it became subject to attacks leveled against postwar urbanization and city form. Hence, the campus can be evaluated through two urbanistic lenses: as a component of the large urban renewal project of the midcentury and as a specific piece of urban design within that project. Within three decades of its opening, its walkways and Forum—key symbols of the new city for which it was built—would meet the wrecking ball.

Campus Revolt

Designed in the early 1960s, UICC opened at a pivotal moment for American universities. Walter Netsch's design sought to incorporate many trends in higher education at the time, particularly the desire for greater inter-disciplinarity, flexibility, and expansion. Yet he could not anticipate the oncoming revolts within American campuses themselves. Many of the factors that led to the campus-building boom of the 1960s also led to an era of national questioning as baby boomers coming of age began to protest against what they perceived to be an increase in the homogenization, mili-tarization, and bureaucracy of American culture and of the universities that represented it. Although much of the collective memory of campus radical-ism in the 1960s and early 1970s focuses hazily on antiwar protests, sev-eral of the most significant protests of the period had to do with the nature of the university itself.

The idea to structure the campus on functional rather than disciplin-ary organization reflected a new stage in the development of the modern university. Clark Kerr, the president of the University of California system, would, in his famous Uses of the University lectures at Harvard (1963), call this new university the "multiversity." The multiversity, Kerr stated, is "an inconsistent institution: responding to and containing multiple communi-ties without a 'single animating principle.'"[3] Kerr understood changes to American higher education and the development of the multiversity within the context of postwar changes to the American economy, in particular the rise of the "knowledge industry," citing statistics illustrating that "produc-tion, distribution, and consumption of 'knowledge' in all its forms is said to account for 29 percent of gross national product."[4] We have already seen how the restructuring of the economy led to an increased *need* for higher educa-tion, but Kerr also recognized the ways in which it was leading to a change in the *form* of education. Kerr's description of the multiversity was built on an analogy with the city:

> The "Idea of a University" was a village with its priests. The "Idea of a Modern University" was a town—a one-industry town—with its intellectual oligarchy. "The Idea of a Multiversity" is a city of infinite variety. Some get lost in the city; some rise to the top within it; most fashion their lives within one of its many subcultures. There is less sense of community than in the village but also less sense of

confinement. There is less sense of purpose than within the town but there are more ways to excel. There are also more refuges of anonymity—both for the creative person and the drifter.[5]

Kerr did not lament the passing of former structures of university life; rather, he sought to understand how the multiversity would change students, faculty, university governance, relations to government and industry, and ultimately society at large. Not all members of the multiversity were pleased with his prospectus.

University of California students were among the first to dissent. The free speech movement on the Berkeley campus in 1964 began in reaction to the university's refusal to grant space for protests and meetings on university property.[6] Mario Savio, perhaps the movement's best-known leader, launched accusations at Kerr that illustrate the extent to which students (and some faculty) were beginning to express deep consternation at the university's alliance with national agendas, be they defensive, economic, or cultural:

> Now, I ask you to consider: if this is a firm, and if the Board of Regents are the board of directors, and if President Kerr in fact is the manager, then I'll tell you something: the faculty are a bunch of employees, and we're the raw material! But we're a bunch of raw material[s] that don't mean to have any process upon us, don't mean to be made into any product, don't mean to end up being bought by some clients of the University, be they the government, be they industry, be they organized labor, be they anyone! We're human beings![7]

What Kerr saw as an opening up of opportunity, others came to see as a closing down of independence. But many of the forces that led to both the bureaucratization of education and the revolts against it would also spur its diversification in type, student base, curriculum, faculty, and research concerns.

Because many campus protests had at their root students' questioning of their institutions' roles in the modern project—mass culture, corporate organization, and military research, for instance—several well-known urban protests and riots of the period had direct ties to university expansion into urban neighborhoods. Here the issue was not the student's place within the institution, but the institution's place within and role in shaping urban space. Proposals to destroy slum housing for a new campus of the

New Jersey College of Medicine and Dentistry were part of the background for the 1967 riots in Newark. A component of Columbia University's student strike in 1968 was the students' opposition, in alliance with the local community, to their university's expansion into Morningside Park.[8] People's Park in Berkeley is another remnant of such conflicts, as the site of riots in 1969 that occurred after the university tore down neighborhood housing to make way for athletic fields. Protests both within the campus and against its expansion would ultimately affect the way universities would interact with surrounding communities.[9]

Reassessing Urban Renewal

As evidenced by the protests initiated by Florence Scala and her neighbors, even as buildings and communities were being razed so that the land beneath them could be prepared as a fresh surface on which to build the renewed city, their inhabitants, architectural and urban critics, and even some politicians were beginning to question the logic and methodology of the process. By the late 1960s, these kinds of reflections on the development of American cities in the post–World War II period would begin to have an impact on the thinking of urban planners, designers, and architects so that by the early 1980s, a full-blown reappraisal of American cities was under way. Areas once seen as "slums" were being reoccupied by new "urban pioneers," the architecture and planning of public housing and expressways were being called into question and in some parts of the country were being torn down, and large-scale urban projects such as UICC were being reappraised. This larger critique of urban renewal under modernistic urban planning principles is best exemplified in the writings of Jane Jacobs. Jacobs's *Death and Life of Great American Cities* (1961) is best remembered today as an ode to her West Village Street in Manhattan, but her purpose was to analyze the effects of forced displacement of urban residents for public housing, highways, and large urban redevelopment projects and the increasing homogenization of urban life caused by planning focused more on the problems of traffic and transportation than on the urban population.[10] Although Jacobs was a well-established architectural journalist, her writings on the failures of postwar American urbanism were touted as a "common woman's" response to elitist professional planners and architects. As an urban citizen, she organized neighborhood protests that put an end to Robert Moses's plan for a crosstown expressway through lower Manhattan, and in so doing she helped inaugurate the movement for neighborhood involvement in urban planning decisions. What urban sociologists and after them urban planners labeled "slums" she called "diverse," criticizing professionals for their inability to handle urban untidiness. She documented the fact that "renewal" rarely solved the problems of specific urban neighborhoods or their inhabitants; rather, renewal programs served the greater economic and political interests of developers and government officials. Rather than bringing people together, she argued, the functionalist city worked against the hybridity necessary to maintain active urban environments.

Reporting on Chicago's great urban proposals in the May 1962 issue, *Architectural Forum* took note of growing neighborhood resistance to urban renewal: "As in many other cities, there has been growing opposition to large-scale clearance and relocation practices—one reason why the city is now stressing neighborhood revitalization and conservation." In the same article, the journal reported that since 1947 (and anticipated to be completed by 1965) the city had undertaken twenty-six clearance projects on 928 acres, requiring the relocation of 43,000 persons.[11] Florence Scala and her neighbors were not alone in their protests over urban renewal in their neighborhood, even if their purpose—to block the building of the campus, not the teardowns themselves—was differently motivated. The failure of the campus design to address the interface with the surroundings, the remaining neighborhoods in the conservation district, only served to prolong university–city tensions. This situation was exacerbated when the design for a hedge around the campus was value-engineered down to a brick wall, signifying that the campus was not of the community; walkways designed to speed students above and across local traffic similarly kept them off neighborhood sidewalks.

Aerial images of Chicago Circle and the expressways that flow into it provide perfect examples of the dislocations created by urban growth in the mid-twentieth century, growth in which arteries designed to spur broad connections created localized physical rifts. In *All That Is Solid Melts into Air*, the political scientist Marshall Berman traced this dichotomy at the root of American modernity. His most poignant experience of this process was the destruction of his own Grand Concourse neighborhood by the building of the Cross Bronx Expressway:

> So often the price of ongoing and expanding modernity is the destruction not merely of "traditional" and "pre-modern" institutions and environments but—and here is the real tragedy—of everything

most vital and beautiful in the modern world itself. Here in the Bronx . . . the modernity of the urban boulevard was being condemned as obsolete, and blown to pieces by the modernity of the interstate highway.[12]

UICC, tethered to the region's new highways, and, indeed, initially named after their intersection, was a clear demonstration of the physical rift Berman described, the creation of an "expressway world" that cuts through or flies over the actual space of the city, its streets and public spaces (Figure 6.1). Reflecting on the French street revolutions of the 1960s, in which students took to the streets in protest against their universities (American students shut down the operations of their campuses but not the entire city), Berman recognized streets as *the* place for political action, spaces of difference. As he described it, echoing the theories of the French philosopher and sociologist Henri Lefebvre, urbanism is a "spatial practice," a way of occupying and living in the city, not simply an abstracted problem of planning or design. Lefebvre, writing in response to the street protests in Paris in 1968, stated, "We should perhaps here introduce a distinction between the *city,* a present and immediate reality, a practico-material and architectural fact, and the *urban,* a social reality made up of relations which are to be conceived of, constructed or reconstructed by thought."[13] Thus, modern zoning was "responsible—precisely—for fragmentation, break-up and separation under the umbrella of a bureaucratically decreed unity."[14]

The urban problems that would come to be associated with the UICC campus, like those Lefebvre associated with modern urban planning, went beyond form to what the campus said about social relations in the city, changed by a shift from the urban fabric of the grid to the circulatory criteria of the highway and the demolition associated with the practices of urban renewal. In the late 1960s, UICC students would find it difficult to take over the chancellor's office, as it was located on the twenty-eighth floor of the administration tower, but the Forum would serve as a convenient place for revolutionary spectacle, distant from the streets of the Loop where Scala and her community activists had marched earlier in the decade (Figure 6.2).[15]

Critique of the Modern City

The reaction to the impact of the campus on its immediate context cannot be untethered from the reaction to the design of the campus itself.

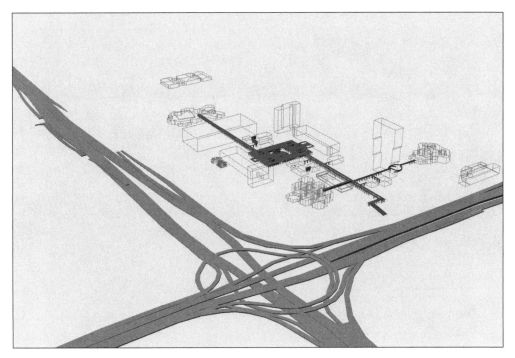

FIGURE 6.1 *Diagram of the Forum and walkways of the UICC campus in the early 1970s (not all buildings in this plan were completed).*

Architecture's complicity in the failures of urban renewal—particularly public housing—became a cause célèbre in 1972 with the famous dynamiting of Minoru Yamasaki's Pruitt–Igoe housing complex in St. Louis, Missouri. Peter Blake's *Form Follows Fiasco* of 1977 is just one of numerous books that used the image of the housing complex's destruction to herald the demise of modern architecture and design and their perceived destructive impact on American cities. Other authors, notably Charles Jencks in his *Language of Post-Modern Architecture* of 1977, would use the event as a marker of the beginning of a return to premodern architectural and urban forms and styles, providing a precedent for a new period of building demolition—now of modernist buildings—and helping generate a movement that would significantly affect later additions to and revisions of the UICC campus.[16]

From these critiques of urban renewal through the methodology of neighborhood demolition, we can move on to a critique of the mechanisms of "synoptic objectification" of the city, the way in which "scopic regime(s) of control, authority, distance, and cool instrumentality" affect our understanding of and attitude toward the making of urban space.[17] Urban theorist

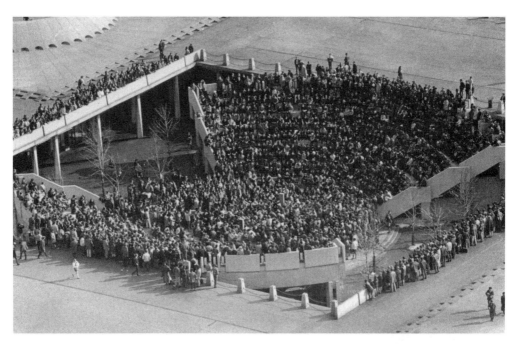

FIGURE 6.2 *Chicago Seven defense attorney William Kunstler speaking to students in the Circle Forum, fall 1969. Courtesy of George Philosophos/Office of the UIC Historian.*

Christine Boyer, in speaking of the urban planning of this period, suggested how a city understood through its neighborhoods became a city understood through its systems:

> Simple linear relationships that had once tied neighborhoods to the metropolitan whole were now understood to be embedded in complex causal networks and subtle behavioral relationships that marked the human and material systems that the city mirrored. It was no longer understanding the urban physical form but the inter-dependent processes that linked yet one more element to another that directed the planner toward more effective interventions in urban development.[18]

Critiques of modern urbanism and critiques of the campus readily paralleled one another. Like the highway systems being built at the same time, UICC was not embedded or integrated into its neighborhood context.

The Circle campus was built during the last moments of utopian modernism in the belief that particular architectural forms could produce particular human responses, societies, interactions, and communities. In the post-industrial, scientifically rationalized city, change would be handled through the production of a multiplicity of forms to address all possible futures—the world could be rationalized through rational form. UICC was a monument to that belief. John Morris Dixon's *Architectural Forum* feature article on the campus when it opened in 1965 summarized and praised the process of its design and implementation, which he called a "model of what a twentieth-century city might be."[19] However, although a campus may be analogous to a city, it is not a city. And although it is true that campus and city are homologous—both formed in community in its greatest sense, a coming together for exchange in its simplest—they are not the same thing. This does not mean that they are not integrally related, indeed overlapping, in their interests and effects. Thus, it was as a model of modern urban design that the UICC campus was most criticized, as a city analog that privileged commuters over communication. In ordering the campus by function rather than by discipline, Netsch's design promoted circulation over interaction. To be fair, in Netsch's pedagogical model, students would be interacting in interdisciplinary classes in addition to in space, but as commuters both to and within the campus, rarely staying in one place for very long, they would only come together for brief intervals.

Early critiques of the campus design were rare, and even when they did occur they focused on function over aesthetics. Although the architectural critic M. W. Newman called the new campus "stunning" and praised its openness to the city in contradistinction to the "usual concept of the campus," he quickly found the "bugs in the concrete," both literally and figuratively. Of particular note were the odd window dimensions and the question of the open walkways in Chicago's cold-weather climate. He quickly recognized two significant features of urbanistic consequence: the wall separating the otherwise outwardly focused campus from its community, and the urban symbol, University Hall. The former became the source of the nickname "Fortress Illini," designating the unresolved relationship between the university and its neighbors. The latter, perhaps reflecting the brewing antagonism between university administrators and students, was already nicknamed "the ivory tower." Newman also identified an inherent conflict in the design, the reflection of the idea of the commuter in the campus's form. Thus, referring to the campus design, he stated, "Around and about are a handsome interplay of big and middle-sized buildings, garden courts, chatter pits—many vistas of geometric combustion that shape horizons out of flatland. It's all vivid and handsome—a one-of-a-kind campus—and will get even better as landscaping and other refinements are added."[20] These are the sensibilities suggested earlier by former student Arlene Norsym. But Newman left open the questions of the campus's success: "Is Netsch's design a true and appropriate academic setting? How much distance, if any, do we want between town and gown? These may be controversial questions as long as this non-ivy commuter's campus is with us."[21] Such concerns were also presented in contemporary writing regarding higher education. The Harvard sociologists Christopher Jencks and David Riesman derided commuter campuses for their failure to promote the student–student and student–faculty interaction that "encourages collective emancipation." They concluded, "Even a superb academic program is unlikely to move most students very far if they return every night to home and mother."[22] Nevertheless, many of UICC's early matriculants were pleased to have an affordable four-year college within commuting distance of their homes and jobs, even if it meant sacrificing the community often associated with the residential college experience.

Despite its pragmatic origins, embedded in UICC's pedagogy and functioning was a utopian vision: the provision of an urban space of education for the city's inhabitants, a project that would stem urban blight and, more importantly, lead to "social renewal." For unlike the urban skyscrapers and suburban office parks of Skidmore, Owings & Merrill (SOM), built for government bureaucracies and capitalist corporations and seen as a "betrayal" of the ideology of modernism, the UICC campus was a truly urban utopian project, the opportunity to build, de novo, an environment that would enable new forms of social and psychological interaction, utilizing new building blocks and technological capabilities.[23] The failure of the modernist city, carried out via urban renewal and functional determinism, exhausted the modern project of historical, social, and cultural progress in general and modern architecture and urbanism in particular. Architectural theorist Anthony Vidler noted in the late 1970s, as early reactions to the effects of both modernism and modernization coalesced, that

> the Post-Modernist age has, we are continually reminded, no such faith in the laws of historical development, nor so strong a belief in the authenticity of abstraction as the basis of modern expression. As the utopia of the Modern Movement has come under social attack, so its aesthetic has been criticized as lacking those dimensions

FIGURE 6.5 *New Forum at the center of the original lecture centers soon after construction in the 1990s. Courtesy of UIC Photo Services (C1.61.06).*

Like modern cities, the modern campus cannot be readily returned to a premodern condition, and as a consequence, struggles with both the campus and its articulation with its urban environment continue to this day.[33]

Many changes in the campus's form came with changes to the university's mission. In combining what became known as the "East Campus," the original UICC, and the "West Campus" (that is, the Medical Center), UIC soon became a Research I institution based on the diversity of its program and degree offerings and the scale of its research budgets. By its twenty-fifth anniversary in 1990, there were concerns that the university was shortchanging undergraduate students and abandoning its accessibility to urban minorities.[34] At the same time, in reembracing its urban foundation under the title "Great Cities Mission"—which highlights the university's programs to build cities and enhance urban life—the university began to reconnect to the Chicago region through service and educational activities, emphasizing the urban-focused research of many of its faculty, colleges, and centers.

Some of these changes clearly reflect changes in the region's demographics.

Forty years after the opening of the campus, the city's population has declined by over 400,000, while its metropolitan region (Chicago-Naperville-Joliet census area) has swelled by well over 2 million, with particular growth in counties farther from the city. Commute times to the campus no longer match those that were used to study potential campus locations, despite the fact that Chicago remains at the center of its region. But as we will see in chapter 7, changes to the commuter status of the campus are also indicative of changes in the expectations of matriculants, who want both an "urban experience" and a "sense of place" from their collegiate years. So too, changes to the mission reflect changes to the economy of the city and to its place in globalization, which also will be explored in chapter 7. More important than the debate over the architectural merits of either the original or the redesigned campus are a series of questions that the redesign of both the university and its campus sidestep, but that persist and affect other campuses and their cities around the country: What is the proper form for the urban campus of the twenty-first century? What is the role of the university in forming the city? Should institutions and projects such as UIC be nostalgic for the past or open to a hybrid milieu?

7

City as Campus: University Space in the Global City

*Their actions are worthy of being called city planning, because
they involve a lot more than the creation of university buildings.
Today, universities find that if they want to build at all, they must
build entire neighborhoods, neighborhoods that provide jobs, housing, services, and entertainment for residents who may have no
academic connections.*

Robert Campbell, "Universities Are the New City Planners," 2005

Along with challenges coming from within academia, new technologies
and research opportunities, global economics, and urban dynamics—
including new movements to revitalize cities—are putting pressures on
urban campuses not only to expand but also to engage in large-scale real
estate development.[1] In the 1990s, the group of industries categorized as
education and knowledge creation ranked second in the United States, after
business services, in the number of jobs added, as most manufacturing industries continued to decline. As one report on cities and their universities stated, "In many respects, the bell towers of academic institutions have
replaced smokestacks as the drivers of the American urban economy."[2] As
Robert Campbell noted, this new standing not only reflects the extension
of the academic mission of universities but also acknowledges their critical
place in making cities the centers of the global economy:

In a way, universities are the industries of today. They've replaced
the manufacturing that has almost disappeared from US cities. A
university imports raw material in the form of 18-year-old minds
and bodies, processes that material, and four years later ejects a
finished product that is ready for the market. Education is today's
equivalent of the production line. It's an economic boon to any city.[3]

Many academics might be troubled by Campbell's instrumental analysis—certainly, Mario Savio would be—but it would appear that most cities
are not. Cities are willing to take the risk of accommodating the expanding

power of universities in exchange for access to their capital, managerial skills, and initiative, which their own agencies, hampered by decreased federal and state funding, years of postindustrial decline and disinvestment, and a loss of public trust, cannot bring together. Increasingly, nonprofits, business groups, and governmental agencies are pushing universities to capitalize on this potential: "[Colleges and universities] are enduring components of urban economies and can become leaders in enhancing urban vitality. Though there are initial efforts, much more can be done to redirect colleges and universities to strengthening our cities."[4] At one time a growing town might have competed to attract a new college to its center, as New Haven did for Yale in the early eighteenth century, and others may have built institutions to advance the training of teachers and preachers, as was the case with Cambridge and Harvard in the seventeenth century, but today's cities are doing more than that; they are actively encouraging higher education not only to spark growth but also to carry it out. If knowledge production in all its varied forms—economic, cultural, scientific, and social—is the key mission of the university and simultaneously critical to urban growth and revitalization, how do campus and urban forms reflect this interrelationship? What new spatial practices are emerging from this fusing of missions? This is where campus planning and design and urban planning and design begin to coalesce.

Certainly, we can recognize how globalization has led to a rebalancing of winners and losers as cities compete to remain or become centers of global networks of capital, but what role has it played in higher education, and how has it affected campus forms? The pressure to keep up with technological, pedagogical, and demographic changes in academia motivates universities to implement new building programs: for new student centers, new dormitories and old dormitory reconfigurations, library modifications to accommodate digital facilities and the staff and equipment that serve them, the wiring of dorms and other campus buildings for Internet connections or provisions for wireless communication, classrooms that can utilize new instructional technologies, gyms and recreational facilities, and parking and traffic accommodation. Additionally, if research universities are to compete for students, faculty, staff, grants, and contracts, they need new medical centers and an expanded array of research facilities. These needs are particularly acute at urban universities, where expansion remains difficult, communities remain wary of exploitation (even as cities encourage campus growth), and students and their parents weigh the quality of urban life as part of their evaluation of the potential quality of campus life. As universities take on new roles as city planners and developers, they have ever more responsibility in the design of the communities and cities that they transform. Yet if one lesson can be discerned from university–city relationships in the 1960s, it is that universities need to actively communicate and integrate their actions with surrounding neighborhoods, and in so doing redefine their relationships with their host cities. Chicago, its urban fabric permanently transformed by both the decline of industry and reactions to this decline, has been drastically reshaped, and universities have played a key role in this process. As the city maneuvers to maintain a position in the global, information-based economy, its campuses have continued to grow and change amidst a new period of urban reconfiguration.

Campus Chicago

The contemporary assemblage of institutions of higher education in Chicago (Figure 7.1) is indicative of the way in which town-and-gown relationships have expanded to include traditional categories of "research, teaching, and service" and new external responsibilities to the urban economy and for the physical revitalization of the city's neighborhoods. In return for this expanded mission, universities have the ability to enlarge their facilities and to pursue further opportunities that are directed back toward the academic community. The expansion of these relationships leads to an intersection of the needs and goals of both the city and the academy "on the ground" (in neighborhoods and communities) and within a "global network" (the space of exchange of goods, services, knowledge, information, an international elite, and large migrating groups). As with all intersections, some result in expanded opportunities for all involved, and others lead to further conflict.

Although not a "first tier" economic global city, such as New York, London, or Tokyo, Chicago is a world city from the perspective of immigration, culture, control of capital, and command over a vast region of agricultural and industrial production.[5] Its universities participate in the global economy through the work produced on their campuses. As Arjun Appadurai noted, the academic world participates in its own forms of "knowledge transfer" throughout a global network of scholars. These flows of information may not have a significant physical presence, but the institutions that house these scholars and their work do.[6] With particular regard to the campus's situation in the city, Chicago is part of a national and worldwide network of touristic cities, many of which are former industrial centers, whose economic vitality is increasingly

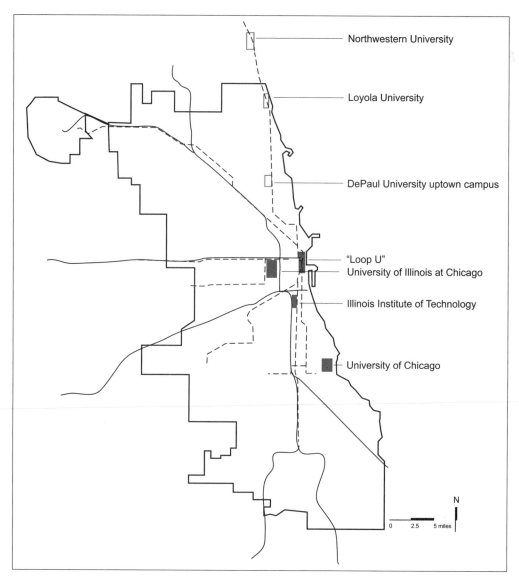

FIGURE 7.1 *Locations of major universities in Chicago at the beginning of the twenty-first century.*

tied to their architectural, cultural, and recreational facilities and their neighborhood vitality. To the extent that university campuses contain and maintain many crucial elements of the touristic city—architecture, museums and galleries, performing arts programs, and sports teams—they contribute to this vital part of the urban economy.

Known as the "city of neighborhoods"—created by immigrant and migrant

FIGURE 7.2 *Adler and Sullivan's Auditorium Building (1889), a National Historic Landmark on Michigan Avenue, now the central building of Roosevelt University.*

Illinois Institute of Technology

Issues as diverse as safety, local housing availability, retail opportunities, the functioning of neighborhood institutions, and the physical deterioration of the campus and its surrounding context can lead to declining enrollment, faculty flight, and a crisis that has at its root the dynamics of the city–campus relationship. In many cases around Chicago, concerns that arose in the post–World War II period remained unresolved or intensified in the late twentieth century. A case in point is IIT, which, owing to the combination of its location and design and its architectural legacy as the center of Miesian modern architecture, has been a focal point for the discussion of the simultaneity of the projects of campus and urban revitalization.

Despite the promises of modern urban design, as exhibited by Ludwig Mies van der Rohe's design for the IIT campus, and the promulgation of this vision, as carried out through the auspices of urban renewal, the IIT campus remains mired in a struggling urban neighborhood. The combination of tabula rasa logic and segregationist impulses that led to the building of the nation's largest assemblage of high-rise public housing projects (and later

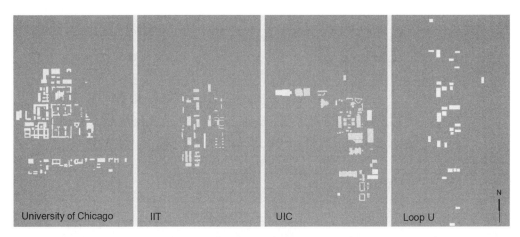

FIGURE 7.3 *Scale comparison of the current University of Chicago, IIT, UIC (East and South campuses), and Loop U campuses.*

to the lack of maintenance required to keep them viable) and the clearance of land for large-scale institutional projects meant that the building of IIT did not bring about the envisioned renewal of this South Side neighborhood in the middle of the twentieth century; instead, they exacerbated already existing problems of decline and disinvestment.

IIT's new vision for its campus is a response to a crisis of faith, in particular in the ability of the institute to continue its pedagogical and research missions within its South Side setting. In 1995, working with its board of trustees, which included a number of prominent Chicago families, businessmen, and funders, the institute recommitted to its location through the commissioning of a master plan by Lohan Associates. The master plan recommends new campus facilities, the maintenance and renovation of the midcentury campus (including both its buildings and its landscape), the provision of new student housing and facilities, and stronger physical connections to the surrounding neighborhood. At the same time, but separately, after decades of corruption, mismanagement, and disinvestment in its public housing stock, the Chicago Housing Authority (CHA) started to take advantage of federal funding to demolish high-rise public housing and to replace some of it with lower-density, mixed-income neighborhoods. Although the projects of the institute and of the CHA are directed toward different constituencies, there is some hope that this coupling will bring a measure of stability to a neighborhood only a short distance from the city's thriving downtown.

The best-known component of the new campus plan is a single building plan to guide its physical development in the first decades of the twenty-first century through landscape programming and new residential, cultural, recreational, and academic buildings designed to reinforce the reading of the territory of the campus within the Hyde Park community. The University of Chicago's master plan is notable for two somewhat opposing themes: on the one hand, a clearer identification of the institution's disparate physical components as part of the campus and academic community, and on the other, despite the fact that the university is continuing to grow physically, the allaying of its neighbors' fears of further urban renewal and gentrification. As we have already seen, the University of Chicago is a clear demonstration of the way in which urban research universities began to sprawl into neighboring communities, while the previously vacant property surrounding them was filled in by residential and commercial development. Students and faculty are so extensively woven into the surrounding community that it is difficult to differentiate where each begins and ends. To the thinking of administrators and trustees, this intertwinement presents a problem of identification for their institution at a time when campus image and space have become an essential measure of institutional quality.

As a result of the university's desire to create a distinct campus, the new master plan returns to the original nineteenth-century campus design, creating localized quads, particularly in new dormitory development, that clearly define student-centered areas and reassert the university's commitment to neo-Gothic architecture as representative of the ideas and mission of the institution.[15] New residential development within the campus signifies one of the biggest ideological aspects of this plan: to bring student life back into the confines of the academic community. Several new dormitories are under development. The first to be completed was the Max Palevsky Residential Commons. Designed by the Mexican firm Legorreta Arquitectos (with the Chicago firm VOA Associates, 2002), this new complex houses over seven hundred students. As suggested by the master plan, the building runs a full block, enclosing a previously open space around the Regenstein Library, a 1970 building by Walter Netsch that is currently being enlarged through an underground expansion by the architect Helmut Jahn.[16] Additional new buildings include the Gerald Ratner Athletics Center (Cesar Pelli & Associates with the Chicago firm OWP&P, 2003), the Charles M. Harper Center of the University of Chicago Booth School of Business (Rafael Viñoly Architects, 2004) (Figure 7.6), and the Reva and David Logan Center for Creative and Performing Arts (Tod Williams Billie Tsien Architects, in design). While advancing the

FIGURE 7.6 *The Charles M. Harper Center of the University of Chicago Booth School of Business (Rafael Viñoly Architects, 2004). The building on the left, across the street from the business school, is Frank Lloyd Wright's Robie House (1909). Tour groups—such as in the Chicago Trolley tour bus passing by—visit both buildings on a Sunday afternoon.*

logic of Henry Ives Cobb's original campus, several of these new buildings attempt innovation in architecture, signaling the desire of the university to use signature architects to revive the architectural image of the campus while expanding the discourse of architecture itself.

Over the next twenty years the university envisions building out the campus on its northern edge to develop a clear boundary along Fifty-fifth Street, filling in empty parcels of land on its South Campus along Fifty-ninth Street with new student housing and facilities (Figure 7.7), and completing the extensive build-out of its Medical Center. The majority of building is occurring on land already owned by the university, much of it acquired during its expansion in the middle of the twentieth century, as discussed in previous chapters.[17] The South Campus development is most likely to stir up debate and is being closely monitored by community activists in the Woodlawn neighborhood, which has not seen the same level of development and gentrification as Hyde Park. The university initiated dialogue in a letter to the Woodlawn community in 2004, and it now maintains active updates to its plan on its Web page "South Campus Planning":

> Over the next 15 years, the University's South Campus will be redeveloped and enhanced with a new student dormitory, additional parking and office space, and, hopefully, small convenience retail. For the first phase of redevelopment, planned changes to the South Campus are consistent with local planning and zoning laws;

however, your input is important to us, especially those of you who live adjacent to the South Campus's southern border, 61st Street. A discussion with you regarding the South Campus gives us an opportunity to work together on important quality of life issues, helping to make this a win-win for the University and for you as a Woodlawn community resident.[18]

The new development along Sixty-first Street is an important interface, as the university desires to create an urban environment and amenities for its facilities south of the Midway Plaisance, while simultaneously shoring up its edges. This reurbanizing of the campus edge is a new approach to designing urban campus communities. The University of Chicago master plan states that as buildings are developed on the long stretch of land between the Midway/Sixtieth Street and Woodlawn/Sixty-first Street, "new buildings will reshape the campus and *enclose it* for the first time, while they *ease the transition* to the redeveloping Woodlawn neighborhood" (emphasis added).[19] The architecture of this "enclosing" and "transitioning" remains to be defined, and as the program of this edge is not fully fleshed out, how the university "converses" with its neighbors to the south, through new retail activity, will define the nature of campus and community interactions for years to come.

The university views its architecture as instrumental to "the unity of the campus and . . . the perfect symbol of the interdisciplinary university." For the campus, Gothic architecture operates as a variable framework to create "places defined by the formal enclosure and containment of the quads."[20] Here "Gothic" is not a style or motif but a strategy of planning that encourages boundaries between the campus and its context, with interaction occurring at specific "portals and passageways." Within the historical quadrangles, a team of landscape architects under the direction of Sasaki Associates is working to reinvigorate the neo-Gothic campus through principles developed by the early-twentieth-century landscape architect Beatrix Jones Farrand. Returning, perhaps, to the 1950s master plan by Eero Saarinen, an even larger effort is underway in the Midway Plaisance on land that belongs to the Chicago Parks District (CPD). Although the original campus turned its back to this wide boulevard, for the past hundred years, buildings have spread along the north edge and, more sporadically, along the south edge. If the university is to continue to expand within the zone it owns to the south, the Midway must be rethought as a center rather than an edge of campus life. As the master plan states:

FIGURE 7.7 *The University of Chicago South Campus buildings. Eero Saarinen's Laird Bell Law Quadrangle with a new undergraduate residence hall under construction is in the background (Goody, Clancy, 2009).*

The Midway also serves as an entrance to the main campus, framing the majesty of its Gothic buildings from the south, and allowing long perspectives of the individual architectural gems of the South Campus, creations of such noted architects as Mies van der Rohe and Eero Saarinen. The University has long struggled with the physical separation of the South Campus from the main campus, but there is a separation of mood as well: The South Campus is a loose collection of individual buildings, some of which are architecturally distinguished, but the South Campus lacks the compact harmony that characterizes the North Campus.[21]

Working in partnership with the CPD, the university's consultants, Olin Partnership and Wolf Clements and Associates, are developing a plan, inspired by Frederick Law Olmsted's original design, that will include new gardens, recreational facilities, and a winter garden to serve both the university and the community. The campus–city partnership has its tensions, as it is university, not neighborhood, residents who will front this new amenity. Yet the project is illustrative of the extent to which campus planning and revitalization must now directly include areas "outside the walls" in order to accomplish expansion in already densely occupied urban areas.[22]

University of Illinois at Chicago, South Campus

Expansion at the UIC campus, like that at IIT and the University of Chicago, involves enlarging opportunities for residential and other facilities for its students but is taking place through an entirely different model of urbanism: the creation of a "campus town," a development of almost sixty acres of land to provide a neighborhood for campus life. The desired effect of this project, known colloquially as South Campus, is to resituate the 1960s campus within an urban neighborhood. But the long-term effects of the strategies for the development of the original campus require that this neighborhood be (re)built at a scale considerably larger than the reurbanization taking place around Chicago's other campuses.

From an urban perspective, UIC's expansion to its south—encompassing South Campus and a subset of development, University Village—addresses the residual effects of the lack of direct campus–community interface at the southern edge of the campus as built in the mid-1960s. Expressways limit the campus on the north and east sides, and over the past forty years the Taylor Street neighborhood to the west, which was designated as a conservation area, has rebounded, in some part due to the presence of the university to its east and west, the remnant of its "ethnic" (Italian) qualities, the rediscovery of the urban life in the 1990s, and new CHA mixed-income housing.[23] The area to the south of the campus, containing the historic Maxwell Street outdoor market and the remains of the nineteenth-century commercial corridor along Halsted and Maxwell streets that framed it, continued to decline. The reasons for this decline are numerous, but it can be seen as a general result of the end of urban renewal, disinvestment, and isolation. For the university, the land to its south was both a problem and an opportunity, and it began to acquire properties in the mid-1980s, at first expanding outdoor recreational facilities. Master planning for South Campus began in the mid-1990s, and the city moved the outdoor market and several businesses to a new location to the east in 1994, in anticipation of university growth.

Although South Campus anticipates new facilities for the university—to date, new student residences, leased office space, an open space containing a sky-sculpture by the artist James Turrell (2006), a convention center (the new Forum), and parking have been developed—it is really large-scale urban development that includes new campus buildings. In essence, the project is a new residential and commercial district (Figure 7.8), focused on the intersection of Halsted and Maxwell streets. It creates a "neighborhood" for the university, restoring commercial activity to the street and supporting it with a ready-made population. Here 750 students live on (actually near) campus, in the city, with bookstores, convenience stores, cafés, and sandwich shops at their feet. At the same time, University Village, a new private residential district of over nine hundred townhouses, apartments, and lofts, takes up much of the land of South Campus. Residents of University Village may participate in the new local street life, but the real draw of the new community is its accessibility to transportation and the Loop as well as a new shopping center, with Target and other big-box retail developing to the east in the South Loop. As much a real estate project as urban design, the complex development mechanism for South Campus leveraged state-initiated development, private financing, and substantial city buy-in through tax increment financing (TIF) and upgrades to the infrastructure and streetscape along Halsted Street.[24]

What looks at first like a straightforward and successful case of neighborhood revitalization in the service of the university has turned out to be quite controversial on several counts. The first controversy is over the complex political and real estate deals that brought about South Campus, yet to be fully revealed and beyond the scope of this book.[25] In the absence of substantial university facilities, some critics argued that the South Campus TIF was a gift to the developers in cahoots with the city and state. Additionally, residents of Pilsen, a Hispanic community to the south, feared that development would lead to gentrification of their own neighborhoods. Another critique of the South Campus development project stemmed from the fact that it initially resembled urban renewal projects of the past. Early drawings of the project cleared the area of all existing buildings, which were deemed unworthy of preservation by university officials, the developers, and their associated architects.[26] Faculty and preservation groups such as the Maxwell Street Historic Preservation Coalition seriously questioned this position and fought, unsuccessfully, to have the area placed on the National Register of Historic Places. What the university and many others saw as

FIGURE 7.8 *New buildings and plaza at the northern edge of the University of Illinois at Chicago South Campus. Courtesy of UIC Photo Services (DG06.39.230).*

vacant, dilapidated, and underutilized storefronts and buildings, others saw as an important, if frail, remnant of the city's past: its immigrant neighborhoods, family-run businesses, street markets, and blues legacy. Although the area's contemporary existence was marginal at best, its past remained part of Chicagoans' sense of history: "Some said they were losing a piece of history as the wrecking ball moved closer to their doorsteps on the street where blues music blared Saturday and Polish sausages were served up to hungry passersby. Early blues musicians and Jewish immigrants used to gather in the area in the first half of the 1900s."[27] Once again, the university became embroiled in an argument over preservation. But where the nascent preservation movement of the 1960s was focused on landmark buildings such as Hull-House (and even then primarily as examples of prefire Chicago architecture) and not on the neighborhoods in which they sat, today's preservationists recognize the importance of ordinary streetscapes and the diverse heritage and cultures that they housed.

The problem remains: how is one to bring together this fragile urban environment with the twenty-first-century needs of the university? In the end, twenty-one facades were saved for redeployment—a "facadectomy"—in a main street design that evokes nineteenth- and early-twentieth-century architecture through materials, detailing, and streetscape furnishings (Figure 7.9).[28] The new buildings, including new parking structures, are all designed for the twenty-first-century urban dweller, as is the private housing that utilizes historic motifs even though not historic forms, within a reconfigured fabric that emphasizes security and exclusivity. UIC has "re-created" the neighborhood that many thought it had destroyed forty years ago, a design that some have called "Disneyesque." Blair Kamin, the architectural critic for the *Chicago Tribune,* who just a few years earlier had hailed the demolition of Netsch's walkways on the East Campus, stated, "What is at stake on Maxwell Street transcends the street itself. The issue is whether we are going to use bricks and mortar to preserve our memories authentically or whether we are going to allow buildings to become facile exercises in make-believe."[29] But in many respects, this journey into the city's past is not as much the university's failure to see into the future as an extraordinary shift in ideas about continuity and innovation in the city, where the urban image of the nineteenth century—which was often quite unstable and uncomfortable—is used to create a settling and comfortable backdrop for contemporary urban life. The backlash against modern urbanism has led not only to a reinvestigation of the historic urban fabric but also to a

FIGURE 7.9 *"Facadectomy" of buildings along Halsted and Maxwell streets in preparation for the development of the University of Illinois at Chicago South Campus.*

reembracing of its building styles and to imitations of historical motifs in the design of lighting, paving, street furniture, and signage. To walk down what remains of Maxwell Street today, however, is to enter into a world that never existed, a touristic journey through the immigrant's experience of nineteenth-century Chicago, which surely did not include sushi restaurants, coffee bars, or a multideck parking garage.

Writing on contemporary campus architecture and its relationship to urban development projects, architect Frances Halsband criticized them as "stealth" expansion through homogenization, "disguised as extensions of the adjacent city, pieces of campuses constructed by commercial builders, satellite campuses of rented space, and Starbuck's everywhere."[30] Halsband's concerns are on target with regard to the extent to which this expansion process yields architecture that is market driven, middle of the road, and new yet familiar rather than reflective of new thoughts on either campus or urban design. In this model of campus growth, innovation is reserved for development techniques and does not appear in design strategies or new thinking about architecture. Where South Campus currently fails as campus design is in its clear distinction from the campus urbanism of the original 1965 spaces, as if it is set up as a historic counterargument rather than as a respeculation on pedagogy and the city; where it succeeds is in developing a model for integrating student life into the fabric of the city. The measure of the success of South Campus will be the extent to which the residents of University Village, the UIC students, staff, and faculty, and Chicago's citizens can sustain this new community, as they do in neighborhoods such as Lincoln Park, where the DePaul University campus has become largely embedded into the street fabric.

Together, these campuses represent a full range of approaches to university expansion at the beginning of the twenty-first century. The University of Chicago, while remaining true to its campus traditions, attempts to mend a history of university–neighborhood conflict. IIT's McCormick Tribune Campus Center, although ignoring its neighboring community, suggests new ways of thinking about the making of urban space. UIC's South Campus, although hiding behind a veneer of history, is the most forward-looking in its approach to the development of a hybrid urban–university program. Each demonstrates the university's expanding role in producing both campus and urban spaces appropriate to higher education's place in the knowledge economy. By tracing their development over the course of the twentieth century, it has been possible to understand the parallel trajectories of Chicago and its campuses. At the same time, new spaces for knowledge production are beginning to appear outside the confines of the campus, suggesting new ways in which the city and its universities interact in the creation of new urban forms and programs.

Matriculating in the Twenty-First-Century City: Loop U

While IIT, the University of Chicago, and UIC have been engaged in a process of reurbanization of their surrounding neighborhoods, a number of institutions are themselves urbanizing through their expansion in and around the Loop (Figure 7.10). Capitalizing on the attraction of a revitalized downtown area, these colleges and universities are in turn bringing 24–7 activity to an area whose once vibrant stores and businesses had declined. The city's 2002 *Chicago Central Area Plan* for the twenty-first century—a successor document to the earlier Central Area of Chicago (CAC) plans—does not just recognize the density of development in higher education in this area; it promotes it as an important sector of the economic well-being of the city. As the plan notes in "A Crossroads of Ideas: The Education Sector," there were already twenty-two postsecondary schools in the general vicinity of downtown, serving 51,000 students (not including those at UIC), and the highest levels of growth were at Columbia College Chicago; DePaul University, downtown campus; Roosevelt University, Chicago campus; and the School of the Art Institute of Chicago (SAIC), with an expectation that together they would grow 34 percent, from 25,000 to 34,000 students, in the five to ten years following.[31] The area is also home to several large, more vocationally oriented schools, such as Robert Morris College. As these institutions work to solidify their base of more-traditional, full-time, postsecondary school students, their need for residential space is also expected to rise and to bring with it a growth in commercial and service activity catering to the 24–7 youth demographic. This presents a significant change in the physical relationship between higher education and the dense, central, business-focused city.

A more recent study commissioned by the Greater State Street Council and the Central Michigan Avenue Association, *Higher Education in the Loop and South Loop: An Impact Study*, goes into greater detail regarding the economic impact of these institutions, dubbing the Loop and South Loop "the largest college town in Illinois."[32] Notwithstanding the pastoral reference, the report's details are urban; at the time of its writing, educational institutions occupied 7.5 million total gross square feet in forty-one separate locations (two Sears Towers), employed more than 12,000 employees, generated $777 million in direct and indirect economic activity that created 13,500 jobs, provided residential space for almost 3,800 students, and spent significant sums of money on capital projects that provided local construction jobs. The study also elucidates less economically tangible but culturally significant aspects of this collective of institutions of higher education, including the use and retrofitting of at least seven important buildings, from the previously mentioned Auditorium Building to several State Street department stores and Chicago school skyscrapers, buildings of the late-nineteenth and early-twentieth centuries, many by famous, innovative architects of their time. The SAIC and Columbia College Chicago, both schools of art and design, maintain museums, galleries, and performing arts facilities that extend the cultural programming of the area's existing museums and theaters. And although neither the *Chicago Central Area Plan* nor the *Higher Education*

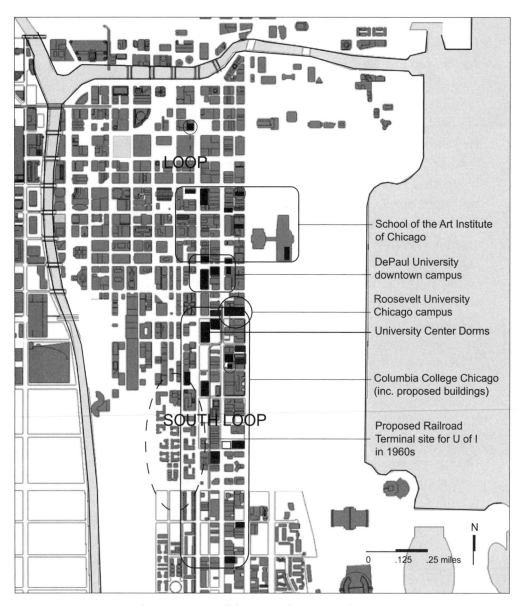

LOOP

SOUTH LOOP

School of the Art Institute of Chicago

DePaul University downtown campus

Roosevelt University Chicago campus

University Center Dorms

Columbia College Chicago (inc. proposed buildings)

Proposed Railroad Terminal site for U of I in 1960s

N

0   .125   .25 miles

FIGURE 7.10 *The "Loop University" district in downtown Chicago.*

study make a direct link between the growth of this "college town" and an increasing number of building conversions and new residential high-rises, the economic and cultural transformation of the area clearly makes it more viable as a residential district for students and nonstudents alike.

In the recommendations for "Education in the Central Area" the *Chicago Central Area Plan* suggests clustering development of academically focused institutions around Congress Parkway, already the center of both Columbia College Chicago and Roosevelt University, as well as the location of the Harold Washington Library Center, the city's central library.[33] This is a critical location between the Loop and the growing residential and commercial area known as the South Loop, the area Mayor Richard J. Daley once hoped to develop by locating UIC on railroad rights-of-way. The plan provides little discussion of the project of the urban university; rather, the focus is on the positive role of these institutions in the preservation and reuse of buildings in the eastern portion of the Loop. As twenty-first-century businesses migrate to the west, where looser preservation conditions allow for the development of large-footprint, high-technology skyscrapers, they leave behind buildings now protected by varying degrees of landmarking.[34] In effect, educational institutions have become the keepers of much of the city's historically important but difficult to utilize nineteenth- and early-twentieth-century skyscraper stock. With their small floor plans but good access to natural light and ventilation, many of these buildings can accommodate faculty offices, classrooms, and residential spaces. Former department stores along State Street, with their deep but flexible floor plans, have also been taken over by these institutions. The most heralded renovation is DePaul's rehabilitation of the former Goldblatt's department store (Holabird & Roche, 1912) into a multiuse building that links to several older buildings in the university's downtown base. Roosevelt University occupies not only Adler and Sullivan's Auditorium Building at Congress and Michigan avenues but also the Gage Building (1899), another historic Michigan Avenue building designed by Holabird & Roche, with a facade by Louis Sullivan. Columbia College Chicago has renovated the landmarked Ludington Building (1891) designed by William Le Baron Jenney (Figure 7.11), one of the city's early steel-frame and terra-cotta buildings. It is currently being used as a student center, gallery space, auditorium, and classroom building.[35] More recently, the SAIC has begun to lease studio space in Louis Sullivan's Carson Pirie Scott Building (1899), one of the city's most famous Chicago school buildings, recently restored after the Carson's department store decided to abandon it as the anchor building of their franchise.

The prescience of the *Chicago Central Area Plan* and the *Higher Education* study lies in the way they understand the Loop institutions as a collective phenomenon, not only rehabilitating historic buildings but bringing innovative programming and purpose to the very heart of the city. That idea would not have been possible in the mid-twentieth century when IIT was built and

FIGURE 7.11 *Columbia College Chicago (historic Ludington Building) streetscape along South Wabash Avenue.*

the location of the University of Illinois at Chicago Circle (UICC) debated. Chicago school–period buildings would not have been considered appropriate for educational use, nor was there a great movement to protect them. Their height did not appear suited to higher education's needs. Further, lack of land for new building would have prevented the construction of a campus precinct, and the mix of uses in the area was too diverse for an appropriate collegiate atmosphere, as it was understood at the time. Richard J. Daley's vision of converting land owned by the railroads in the South Loop into the UICC in his own CAC plan of 1958 was forward looking. Yet that plan was only conceivable because of the potential that a large parcel of vacant land would become available once the railroad terminals were removed, as urban planning and design of the time called for either vacant land or the erasure of existing buildings and neighborhoods to produce a fresh ground for a new form of city. The integration of old and new and the nuanced interweaving of diverse functions were antithetical to modern urban design and to the campuses based on it, such as UICC.

Individually, each of these Loop institutions has a valid reason for its downtown location—accessibility to jobs, cultural institutions, public transportation, and faculty and staff—but it is the intercollegiate activities and partnerships of these diverse institutions that allow them to be conceived as a new form of campus. The new University Center (Figure 7.12), a collective dormitory project of Columbia College Chicago, DePaul University, and Roosevelt University, illustrates how the aggregation, as it is centered at Congress and State streets, can offer amenities and facilities at a scale that none could support alone. The important site, which was worth five million dollars and was sold to a nonprofit developer for one dollar, sits diagonally across from the central library. The University Center (VOA Associates and Antunovich Associates, 2004) houses approximately 2,000 students and provides a host of services for twenty-first-century student life: a fitness center, multimedia rooms, music practice rooms, art studios, game studios, a rooftop garden, and student-oriented retail spaces at grade.[36]

The University Center and the other residential buildings to be found in the Loop resolve a number of problems associated with commuter campuses by bringing students into the twenty-four-hour experience of university life, resolving the security concerns of parents and accommodating the desire to form an academic community that encompasses more than just the space of the classroom. As one Columbia College Chicago student who wanted a more diverse college experience stated, "Some people find downtown to be

FIGURE 7.12 *University Center, a joint dormitory for Columbia College Chicago, DePaul University, and Roosevelt University in downtown Chicago.*

a cultural shock, but I feel comfortable and perfectly safe here."[37] And as Tony Jones, then SAIC president, said of the opening of one of his school's dormitories in the Chicago Building (Holabird & Roche, 1904), "This place makes the whole city [the students'] classroom. We've put them at ground zero [State and Madison streets], the literal heart of Chicago."[38] What the *Chicago Tribune* dubbed "Downtown Chicago U," "the most exciting 'campus' in Illinois," contains advantages that neither traditional nor commuter campuses easily accommodate: the ability to combine facilities for both traditional students (post–high school, residential) and increasing numbers of nontraditional students (older, often second-career students who have a wide variety of off-campus responsibilities) (Figure 7.13).[39]

And Loop U is more than a commuter campus. In addition to the University Center, over the past decade all these institutions have converted Loop buildings into student residence space or built new residences from scratch. The SAIC initiated new student housing development in the late 1990s by building a new residential building and converting adjacent buildings in the North Loop.[40] A Borders bookstore, a food court, and the Gene Siskel Film Center were positive additions to the area, currently undergoing transformation into a theater district. For the institutions themselves, new residential buildings allow them to provide unique facilities such as practice spaces and art studios, which for the art and design institutions are as crucial as libraries to campus life.

The downtown universities do as much for the city as the city does for them; they add vitality and diversity, activating the urban program through new cultural and commercial facilities and animating the ground plane through the twenty-four-hour comings and goings of student residents. The street-facing galleries of the art and design programs replace once empty storefronts, and the presence of students promotes theaters and performance spaces (as well as cafés, restaurants, and some bars). Wherever one turns in the East and South Loop today, one sees students working at laptops in coffee shops and student lounges (Figure 7.14), electronic projections, galleries, and new retail spaces that offer visual, virtual, and physical access into the world of twenty-first-century education. This new campus is not only urban; it is also uniquely interactive and intercollegiate. Nonetheless, with buildings scattered around multiple blocks, the Loop U institutions struggle to maintain a coherent sense of place and urban identity. This problem is particularly acute for Columbia College Chicago, which lacks an anchor building and is stretched out over an area two blocks wide and six blocks long.

FIGURE 7.13 *DePaul University (historic Leiter Building) streetscape along State Street, part of the larger district nicknamed "Downtown U."*

Its 2006 master plan, therefore, promotes the development of a "cognitive" space through new building projects and identity creation, a form of urban branding. The centerpiece of the new buildings is a new campus center located midway between the north and south ends of the campus. Additional new or renovated buildings are set adjacent to existing campus buildings to heighten existing hubs of activity. Building projects are augmented by super graphics (Figure 7.15), sidewalk installations, murals, street furniture, and "arcons" (vertical scrolling LED lights) meant to unite the buildings into a coherent campus district.[41] Columbia College Chicago's campus, similar in size to IIT's campus, is the latter's inverse. Rather than taking a tabula rasa approach to the site to create a base for a new form of urbanism, Columbia College Chicago repurposes existing urban form. Rather than conjoining buildings with fields of green, Columbia College Chicago exists amidst a completed urban fabric. (Rapid development in the South Loop is filling in the remaining open spaces.) Yet this take on the urban campus is not a rejection of the form of the mid-twentieth-century campus. Rather than using nineteenth-century campus form as an intellectual basis for the building of a new piece of the city, the preexisting nineteenth-century city is used as the campus.

Despite the innovative integration of city and campus suggested by Loop U, this development raises a number of questions about insinuating new programs in historic contexts. For instance, the SAIC's dorm by Booth Hansen (2000) at the prominent corner of State and Randolph streets suggests that despite innovations in the building's programming, the institution was not willing to be innovative in its architecture, calling into question its reputation as an institution on the cutting edge of art and design. Hansen's building is a near replica of D. H. Burnham's Reliance Building of 1895 just down the street, which has found a new use as a boutique hotel.[42] Is replication of what was once innovative architecture a valid form of urban preservation, or is it simplistic nostalgia? The same question arises at the University Center, a pastiche of overscaled motifs reminiscent of neighboring Chicago school buildings, but completely different in size and detail.[43] These new buildings allude to unresolved questions in urban preservation: must new buildings in older cities imitate their context through appropriation of their styles?

The movement to preserve but also to imitate the historic motifs of the innovative architecture of the early-modern period has become problematic for the development of contemporary architecture in Chicago. Buildings such as the SAIC dorms and the University Center, like many of UIC's

FIGURE 7.14 *DePaul University student spaces on Jackson Boulevard.*

new buildings on its South Campus, are part of the reaction to midcentury modernism through a return to historical references, again the architecture of the late nineteenth century. They are part of a trend to capitalize on the ideas of historical continuity in the overhaul of the Loop in the mid-1990s, a decision that conjoined economic and physical revitalization with national and international tourism, encouraging educational institutions such as colleges, institutes, and universities to increase their presence in an area previously alien to their activities. At the same time, however, this renovation of the city of the past has served to stifle the kinds of advances in architectural technologies and expressions for which Chicago is well known. And given the reputation that educational institutions have for supporting architectural and design exploration, it is unfortunate that the reaction to modern architecture and urbanism has led them away from more-contemporary design investigations. However, the more one moves from the center of the Loop, the more daring these institutions become. A new dormitory for Columbia College Chicago, also by Booth Hansen, uses an

FIGURE 7.15 *Columbia College Chicago branding in the context of the redevelopment of the South Loop.*

existing South Loop building as a base for an addition and additional floors that are clearly articulated as a new and structurally complex steel-and-glass structure. Columbia College has recently opened a new Media Production Center by Studio Gang Architects, a young Chicago firm, even further to the south, a building that promises not only innovative uses but innovative architectural exploration. And perhaps reflecting a shift in the aesthetic sensibilities of Chicago in the early twenty-first century, a new high-rise, mixed-use campus building for Roosevelt University designed by VOA Associates is under construction adjacent to the Auditorium Building. The architectural critic Blair Kamin likened its "zigzagging profile" to the sculptor Constantin Brancusi's *Endless Column.*[44]

But for the purposes of this study, it is the accumulation of higher education institutions in the Loop and South Loop districts, and not the individual merits of their buildings, that offers insights into new urban spatial practices. Though universities are expanding online research, distance

FIGURE 7.16 *Loop U student studying in front of Roosevelt University (historic Auditorium Building).*

learning, and high-technology teaching techniques, the physical campus—stressing the notion of a community—has not lost its appeal. Further, proximity remains a necessity for urban institutions that are closely tied to their urban settings for the provision of services, jobs, research facilities, cultural resources, part-time and "practitioner" faculty, and social and professional contacts to fill out their missions. As Alicia Berg, then commissioner of the city's Department of Planning and Development and now vice president of campus environment at Columbia College Chicago, stated regarding the University Center project, "Downtown used to be a commuter campus, but now it is becoming a traditional campus."[45] But it is a traditional campus program only programmatically, not urbanistically. Only when students are within the walls of their school's buildings are they truly within their institutions. Beyond that, the city truly is the campus (Figure 7.16).

As Arjun Appadurai wrote, "It has now become something of a truism that we are functioning in a world fundamentally characterized by objects in motion. These objects include ideas and ideologies, people and goods, images and messages, technologies and techniques. This is a world of flows."[46] At the same time, the ability of a city to remain or become central rather than marginalized in this global network requires it to be a site of "production and innovation."[47] In line with the research of economist Saskia Sassen on the importance of proximity in the development of businesses in a global environment, these schools—from small teaching-focused institutions to large research-driven universities—demonstrate the degree to which place still constitutes the conceptual underpinning of the campus, as it does of cities. Sassen views globalization and urbanization through the lens of economics, but her argument that globalization leads to place-based agglomeration as well as functional diversification suggests why the city of Chicago offers not only encouragement but also financial incentives to develop the Loop institutions, many of which specialize in fields such as media and the arts, technology, and the twenty-first-century professions crucial to the city's role in the global network. Where Richard J. Daley saw the establishment of the UICC campus as critical to the preservation of Chicago as the regional city of the mid-twentieth century, his son, Richard M. Daley, equally enthusiastically, if less vociferously, has advocated for "Downtown Chicago U," a reciprocal relationship in which city and campus merge.

Throughout the late twentieth century, the city of Chicago promoted and assisted in the development of higher education within its boundaries. In all these instances, the university and the city have moved well beyond traditional town-and-gown relationships. The evolution of higher education has been important not only in stabilizing neighborhoods but in building them, from the restoration of public spaces like the State Street Boulevard and the Midway Plaisance, to the re-creation of street life on South Halsted or the South Loop, to students' repopulation of moribund business districts. At the same time, universities are expanding and restructuring their own environments. Although new dormitories and their attendant student-oriented amenities return the student to the familial confines of the campus, novel locations such the Loop and UIC's South Campus and hybrid building typologies reconnect them to the ideas and life of the city, its urbanity. In these ways, the space of the campus is neither dominant over nor distinct from the city; in fact, it is fully dependent on and imbedded within urban space.

Conclusion

The principal quality we imagine is urbanity: a place that promotes interaction, among communities of the university, neighborhood and city. In future years, the major advances and breakthroughs in higher education and research will likely occur in the intersection of disciplines, of ways of thinking. Achieving positive relationships with communities also requires understanding the intersections of their goals and the opportunities to meet them.

Marilyn Jordan Taylor, "Crossing beyond the Boundaries:
Columbia University in West Harlem," 2000

arilyn Jordan Taylor's description of the design for Columbia University's new Manhattanville campus could equally describe the qualities of urban space and interaction occurring today in Chicago's South Loop: the interpenetration of campus and city not only enabled by chance location but purposely created and promoted through design.[1] The narrative of the case study of Chicago that forms the core of this book, the story of how its universities have contributed to the production of new urban organizations and ideas and how the city has informed the creation of new campus spaces and forms, is situated within larger national trends as universities expand both their missions and their campuses to meet the needs of twenty-first-century higher education. Here I would like to briefly describe some of these trends and speculate on what the Chicago case may teach us as we move toward campuses conceived around ideas of "urbanity," where campus and city interact across fluid boundaries.

Repairing the Wounds of Urban Renewal

How are today's universities engaged in the production of knowledge around cities and their communities? More and more universities invoke the city or urban life as part of their mission statements; the directive to engage the city sounds simple but can lead to situations that are at once extremely nuanced, highly volatile, and potentially long-lasting in effect. What do universities get in return for their efforts? As Ira Harkavy, founding director of the Center for Community Partnerships at the University of Pennsylvania, stated, "Universities that are seen as problem solvers will be the great universities of the next century."[2] Today's urban universities, Harkavy and his collaborator John L. Pucket claimed, should reunite the two great models of the late-nineteenth-century Progressive movement: the foundation of the urban research university and the work of the social settlements. They argued that the split in these institutions' missions, techniques, and reward systems led to a loss of the potential for truly progressive educational institutions where research, teaching, and public service would be seen comprehensively, and whose mission would be directed toward "societal transformations," particularly those taking place in cities. They did not deny that a university's role in community service might be self-serving, but academically based community service, they argued, returns to the university in knowledge production.[3] This "neo-progressive" approach is itself controversial. It both calls for the university to be a "moral institution" and, in teaching and compelling civic engagement and responsibility, returns higher education to the nineteenth-century model of nation building.[4] It also goes against the grain of the structure of contemporary higher education and the notion that the production of knowledge should be a discrete pursuit, unencumbered by social, political, cultural, or economic forces.

The reform agenda of Hull-House, according to Harkavy and Pucket, accomplished a balance between an internal community and a larger urban community by applying research to address the problems of urban life through both educational programs and studies of the urban environment. I would argue, too, that the spatial organization of the settlement as an institution embedded into the physical fabric and social life of its neighborhood was key to this engagement. The techniques of community building used by Hull-House residents, including the crossing of boundaries between urban living, research, and education, was expressed in architecture in a way that was distinct from the model of urban university campuses being developed almost simultaneously. The exclusionary nature of the university campus compound reinforced the increasing isolation of scientifically defined research from the activist agenda of the reform movement, even as the university built powerful frameworks for understanding and commenting on urban transformation.

Although the nineteenth-century city is an inappropriate design model for the twenty-first-century city and the social settlement is a programmatically inadequate model for contemporary urban engagement and reform, universities are increasingly active in their neighboring communities in ways purposely designed to repair the wounds of midcentury urban renewal by reversing the effects of land-banking by building new housing and creating new community institutions. Many of these projects are simultaneously self-interested and directed toward constituencies beyond the campus community. A few examples serve to underscore the range of these activities. To jump-start neighborhood revitalization, numerous universities are involved in investment in and expansion of existing residential building stock, which simultaneously lures middle-class residents to the community, provides housing for university staff and faculty, and improves the image and safety of the campus context. New Jersey, whose cities suffered significant decline in the 1960s and 1970s, has initiated a statewide College and University Homebuyer's Program aimed at urban neighborhoods surrounding thirteen campuses in six cities.[5] At a smaller scale but using more diverse funding mechanisms, Howard University, a historically black university in Washington, D.C., has been working to revitalize the LeDroit Park Historic District adjacent to its hospital.[6] It combines this residential work with community development, providing libraries and starting a charter middle school for the neighborhood.[7] Of course, such programs are not always benign, as campus neighbors can suffer displacement as their communities gentrify. Mindful of this dynamic, the Ohio State University has taken a different approach. Through a nonprofit community urban redevelopment corporation, Campus Partners, the university has taken over large-scale rehabilitation and redevelopment of affordable housing surrounding its campus for residents who are not associated with the university and has directed land-grant extension work directly into these neighborhoods. According to Stephen Sterrett, director of community relations, Campus Partners has a three-part goal: to "address important issues in the lives of our citizens, generate new research, and offer new ways of learning for our students."[8] In this way, the work of the university outside its campus—even in communities unrelated to the university—is seen to support the traditional university mission of service, research, and teaching.

The University of Pennsylvania's extensive university-driven neighborhood revitalization projects have been the model for many recent programs, including an early homeownership program and funding to purchase, develop, and manage targeted rental buildings. Significantly, in the mid-1990s Penn recognized and began to respond to its own role in the physical decline of West Philadelphia. Under the leadership of then president Judith Rodin, it began extensive projects connecting itself to its neighbors, the large, historic urban neighborhood in which it sits.[9] One of the more novel aspects of Penn's documentation of its projects is the extent to which it has acknowledged its own role in fostering physical town–gown conflict:

> University investment and development decisions over the years had created new barriers between the University and adjacent communities. Urban renewal–era development to the north [of the university] had produced a zone of newly constructed institutionally controlled office and residential facilities designed exclusively for the use of the University population or employees of the University City Science Center. These facilities, constructed on blocks previously occupied by homes and neighborhood-oriented businesses, discouraged interaction between the campus and the community.[10]

The university sees its initiatives as "an *administratively driven* approach that was *academically informed*"—an alternative to the other possibilities: "programming, fortification, and abandonment"—and recognizes that its institutional stability is a potential community asset and that its responsibilities go beyond an academic program.[11] In this regard it has worked with the city of Philadelphia to establish a new elementary school that it helps support through ongoing relationships with university departments. It has also worked with other schools within the greater West Philadelphia area to develop curricula, teacher training, and new partnerships between the university and the public schools. Technologies available within the university, such as the Cartographic Modeling Laboratory that allows the School of Social Work and the School of Design to collaborate on projects using geographic information systems (GIS), have also been utilized for mapping and tracking the status of properties and neighborhoods throughout the city.[12] These efforts are reinforced through design. Enhancing the connection between the campus and the community, current landscape plans by Laurie Olin extend the streetscape of the campus beyond its boundaries. This extension has a practical purpose, uniting disparate campus buildings through a unified (and policed) streetscape, but it serves to illustrate the interconnectedness of the surrounding community and the university. Yet just as universities must "police" their contexts, so too must they be careful to "police" the campus–community interface, as the importance of the contemporary university to urban revitalization places the university in a powerful position vis-à-vis urban decision making and development, a much stronger position than that of its neighbors.

Expanding University

Not only are universities engaged in urban stabilization projects, but they are also undertaking vast expansion projects directed toward large swathes of the city. The primary purpose of such projects is to address the need for expanded and renewed campus facilities, but they often move well beyond immediate university requirements to planning, designing, and developing new urban amenities, neighborhoods, or large districts. Of particular interest here are the ways in which these developments, some extensions of existing campuses, and others new campuses in themselves, reflect novel approaches to architecture and design that suggest new thinking about the physical relationship between town and gown and, in some instances, about building the city that the campus will inhabit. Space does not allow for a comprehensive review of such projects. Here I would like to address two—albeit briefly—to highlight key dimensions in the rethinking of the form of the twenty-first-century urban university: transparency and interdependency, both of which can be seen in prototype form in Chicago's campuses.

Having already exploded well beyond the walls of its early-twentieth-century "urban academical village," Columbia University is now engaged in one of its biggest expansions to date, a new nearly-forty-acre development just to its north and west. Its new Manhattanville campus (Figure C.1), predominantly intended for expanded university functions, inverts the form of its walled Morningside Heights campus. To promote qualities of negotiation and transparency, the master plan preserves Manhattan's street grid, places retail and other neighborhood-focused activities at the ground level (Figure C.2), suggests architectural surfaces of glass and steel, preserves some of the neighborhood's manufacturing buildings for reuse, and leaves a central green space open to the community. Lee Bollinger, Columbia's president, has stressed the novel ideas behind the design: "Morningside is a great academic space, but it would be inconceivable to try to replicate it—to make a place of stone and brick, of gates and walls. The new campus must reflect today's closer relationship of the university with the city."[13] Marilyn Jordan Taylor, one of the architects of Columbia University's Manhattanville project, referred to it as "Campus *and* Not Campus," which speaks both to the physical intertwining of traditional university and urban functions into a single project and to the intellectual interaction that is understood to be the hallmark of the twenty-first-century university. She was quite blunt: "Development of such buildings is bringing nearly all urban universities into contested neighborhood settings."[14] The site, between 129th and 133rd streets, running from Broadway to the Hudson River, is currently zoned for manufacturing and contains approximately 140 apartments. Anticipating the neighboring community's concerns, university officials stress that the new development will create 9,200 jobs and $1 billion in annual spending.[15] As Columbia began to move through New York City's complex approval process in May 2007, David Dinkins, former mayor of New York City and now a professor of public affairs at Columbia, wrote in an op-ed piece for the *New York Times,* "Columbia's Manhattanville proposal [will] gradually create a new kind of open, urban campus that will improve local streets; bring back commercial life to Broadway, 125th Street and 12th Avenue; and better connect the residential areas of Harlem with the waterfront park now under construction along the Hudson River."[16]

The Manhattanville campus plan replicates the qualities that already exist in prototype form in conditions such as Chicago's South Loop or in lower Manhattan, where the buildings of New York University (NYU) share city streets with hybrid urban functions around the public space of Washington Square Park. If built out to its full extent, it will test whether the inversion of campus green and urban fabric can be a successful design methodology for integrating the campus and the city. But although the Manhattanville design uses the structure of city blocks to form the campus, it does not undertake large-scale urban planning. For such a project, it is necessary to look back to one of the country's other early institutions, Harvard University.

Harvard University's proposal for the development of Allston, the Boston community across the Charles River from the university's main campus in Cambridge, is perhaps the most extensive and controversial university expansion underway in the country at this time. The Allston project builds on the kind of real estate development/campus expansion we have already seen in places such as the University of Illinois at Chicago's South Campus. Where it differs—in extreme ways—is in scale and urban purpose. The university owns over 350 acres in Allston, significantly more than its 200-plus acres in Cambridge (Figure C.3); the Allston master plan consists of both twenty- and fifty-year phases, a build-out of urban proportions. What is novel about Harvard's approach is not just the scale of the project, but the

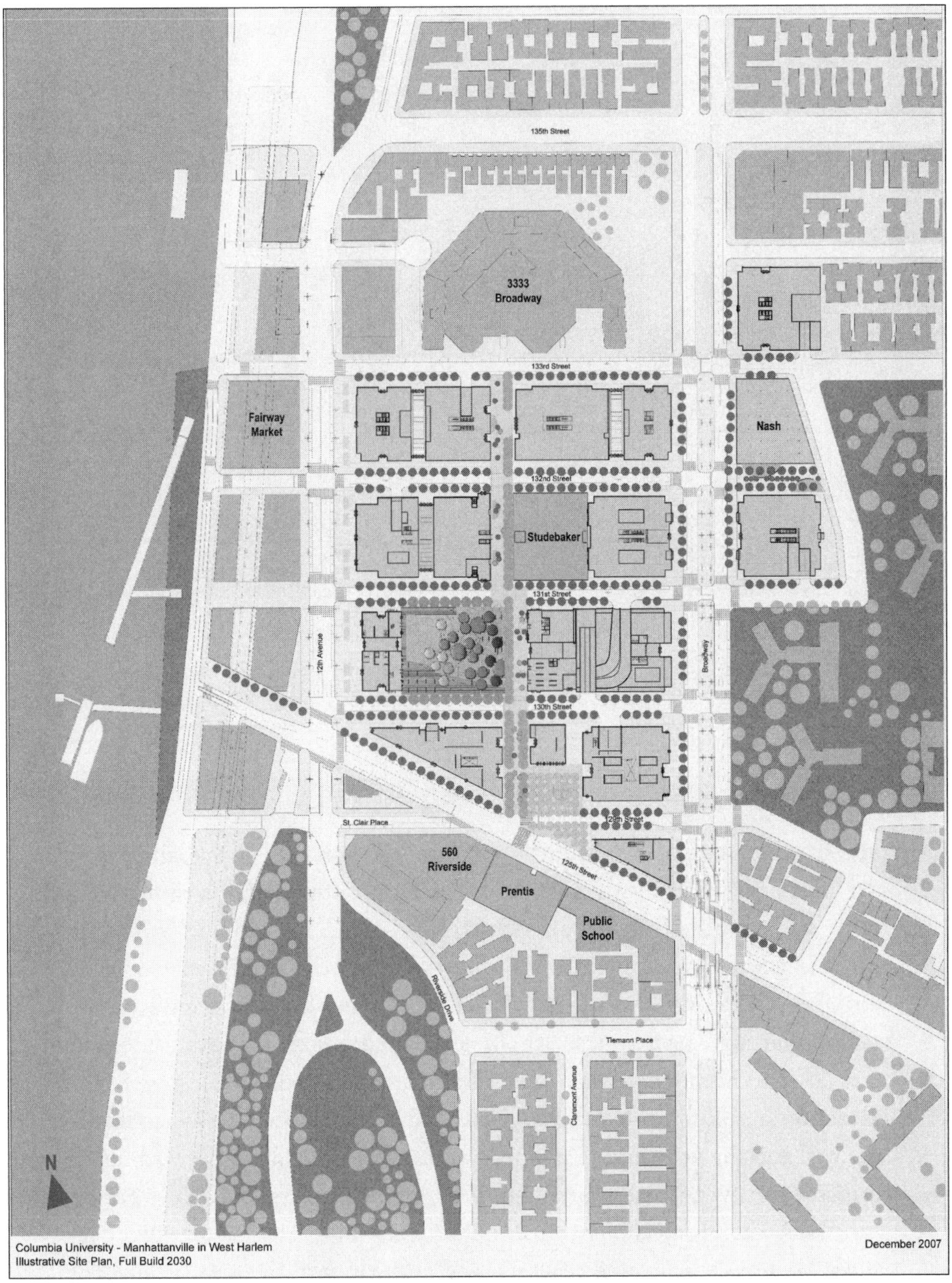
135th Street
3333
Broadway
133rd Street
Fairway
Market
Nash
132nd Street
Studebaker
131st Street
12th Avenue
Broadway
130th Street
129th Street
St. Clair Place
560
Riverside
Prentis
125th Street
Public
School
Riverside Drive
Tiemann Place
Claremont Avenue
N
Columbia University - Manhattanville in West Harlem
Illustrative Site Plan, Full Build 2030
December 2007

FIGURE C.1 *Columbia University—Manhattanville in West Harlem; site plan of 2030 full build-out. Renderings by Renzo Piano Building Workshop, Architects, and Skidmore, Owings & Merrill, Urban Designers; courtesy of Columbia University.*

FIGURE C.2 *Columbia University, Manhattanville campus; preliminary rendering of the view at 131st Street and Broadway looking west. Renderings by Renzo Piano Building Workshop, Architects, and Skidmore, Owings & Merrill, Urban Designers; courtesy of Columbia University.*

fact that the university intends to develop only portions of the land for its own purposes and to use its resources as an economic and design engine for an entire piece of the city. In doing so, it is proposing to perform a task that few if any American cities can carry out themselves. The institutional purposes of the master plan for Allston are to build upon existing facilities such as housing, the Business School, Harvard Stadium, and athletic fields; to develop a campus to accommodate growing professional programs (the Education and Public Health programs); to expand facilities for scientific research and the arts; and to support its student housing needs within the context of a new urban environment built by the university. Equally important, the Allston project envisions a new kind of interdisciplinary university where previously scattered research and cultural facilities can be brought together in a coherent fashion within an emerging city neighborhood.[17]

Two quotations from the public filing of Harvard's master plan illustrate the key theme of this book, that the production of knowledge and the production of urban space are intertwined and have the potential to create new interdependent urban and campus forms:

> Since its founding, Harvard University has advanced knowledge as the needs of society have evolved. Today, this process continues. At a time when society's most complex and pressing problems—from the need to better understand health and disease, to our obligation to improve public education—increasingly require the development of new teaching and research methods, Harvard University is poised to respond.

> Rather than creating an insular and homogeneous academic environment in Allston, the University seeks to develop a mix of complementary uses that foster a lively sense of urban community. Unlike more traditional collegiate settings that clearly delineate between campus and community zones, Harvard seeks to create an open relationship that integrates academic development with civic, neighborhood and public functions.[18]

At Harvard, the success of the enterprise will rely not only on new university buildings, open spaces, and neighborhoods for the use of the academic community, but also on the redevelopment of a large piece of the city for residents with tangential relationships to academia. It will hinge on Harvard's ability to orchestrate the diverse demands of real estate development, urban planning, urban design, and architecture within Boston while advancing the cause of the twenty-first-century global university through design innovation.

Harvard's projects in Allston will go well beyond its own institutional needs to create new civic, commercial, and residential buildings, open space, and streetscapes. The plans address sustainability, transportation planning, new mass transit connections and links to expressways, land remediation, and storm-water management. Development at this scale could require the university to become involved with the building of a new commuter rail stop and with issues surrounding federally subsidized housing.[19] Although still in the design phase and not yet fully approved, current images available through the university's online exhibitions, draft master plans (Figure C.4), and regulatory filings suggest a mixed-use, pedestrian-friendly, villagelike streetscape in contrast to the hard-edged, decaying, industrial quality of today.[20] An

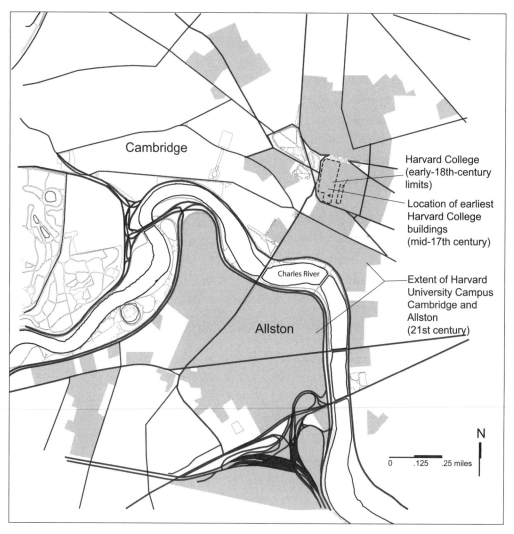

Cambridge

Harvard College
(early-18th-century
limits)

Location of earliest
Harvard College
buildings
(mid-17th century)

Charles River

Extent of Harvard
University Campus
Cambridge and
Allston
(21st century)

Allston

N

0   .125   .25 miles

FIGURE C.3 *Extents of Harvard University's Cambridge and Allston land holdings relative to the early campus of Harvard College (see Figure I.3).*

"academic hub" holds together the disparate assemblage of institutional buildings and links them to a new group of civic buildings and cultural spaces where the university intersects with the existing community. They are linked together not only by streets but by parks, greenways, urban farms, and orchards. By contrast, Harvard's new buildings are designed to reiterate the historic quads of the Cambridge campus within idioms of contemporary architecture, suggesting the university's important role as a patron. They are likely to be designed by today's stars or rising stars of architecture.[21]

FIGURE C.4 *An early master plan for the Harvard University Allston campus, now under revision. Courtesy of Cooper, Robertson & Partners*

By moving graduate and research facilities to Allston, Harvard accomplishes a number of important institutional goals, finding new space for interdisciplinary research and teaching while preserving its own rich campus and architectural legacy and the surrounding historic neighborhoods of Cambridge. Yet the Allston neighborhood is not a blank slate, and it will take decades to determine whether the simultaneous development of university and neighborhood buildings will result in a new form of urbanity.[22] What is clear, however, is that in the Allston plan the historic campus is left behind as a cultural and architectural artifact.

The global economic crisis that marked the end of the first decade of the twenty-first century has had a significant impact on the endowments of the nation's universities; however, it has not forestalled many expansion projects. A number have slowed or been put on hold, but few have been canceled. As of this writing, Columbia University has won an appeal to a court decision that would have prevented the use of eminent domain to obtain land for the Manhattanville campus. The recent ruling noted that the land was "blighted" and that expansion of the new campus "served a public purpose."[23] In early

2010 NYU announced plans to expand its campuses by six million square feet, a 40 percent increase over its existing facilities. A notable aspect of the plan is that although half the expansion is intended for the core campus in Greenwich Village, the remainder will be spread around the city, at the university's medical center but also in Brooklyn, where the university will start a new engineering school with the existing Polytechnic University, and on Governor's Island. On this semiabandoned island south of Manhattan, it "envisions an institute that would unite several academic disciplines around a subject like the urban future. 'What does it mean in the 21st century to build a great city?' [John E. Sexton, the university's president] said. 'Let's be the lab and thinking space for it, the center in the world for thinking about cities.'"[24] Indeed, as local governments struggle to maintain public services in a recessionary economy, the role of the university in creating and maintaining the urban realm becomes increasingly important.

However, not all faculty agree that the new global, networked environment requires university expansion. In recent op-ed articles for the *New York Times* and *Forbes Magazine*, Mark C. Taylor, the chairman of Columbia's Religion Department, took both his own university and others to task for undertaking massive new building projects at a time when higher education is becoming increasingly unaffordable. As part of a larger argument for the reform of higher education, Taylor suggested that globalization and networking should enable increased interdisciplinary exploration and cross-institutional collaboration. Seeming to contradict the institutional argument that growth is a necessary requirement for global competition, Taylor contends that university expansion is but one example of the institutions' inability to "live within their means." He noted, "American higher education has long been the envy of the world, but today our institutions are eroding from within and are facing growing competition from countries like China and India, which are developing ambitious plans to enter the global higher education market."[25] But how do new campus buildings and configurations situate the university within globalization?

Speculations on the Urban Campus in the Age of Globalization

The challenge confronting universities as they plan major expansions is to allow and design for the integration of university and community functions while retaining the "sense of place" associated with American campuses.

Will they build innovative new buildings or replicate historical prototypes? Will they create new urban districts and user interfaces or situate themselves behind new walls and gates? It is my contention that as the university expands the territories of knowledge within academia, it must work along two critical axes outside academia. First, as it produces new buildings and spaces to produce its work, it must recognize that these too are forms of knowledge. It cannot retreat into nostalgia for a past campus space or form; rather, it must exercise its patronage to advance architectural and urban design. Second, it must be mindful of the potential for conflict between the expansion of the urban mission and the expansion of the physical territory of the campus. New campus and urban forms must be found that reinforce and foster rather than work against campus and community interaction.

How these physical articulations with the city and with the communities outside the university's boundaries are accomplished is highly dependent on how the university understands the community within. In the university, the past resides in the present in the form of knowledge, but also through its buildings. Bill Readings's categorization of the modern university as a "ruined" institution modeled on a city, discussed in the introduction to this book, derived from the largely Enlightenment concept of the university as a center for the production of reason to advance a national culture. Toward the end of the twentieth century, as the role of the nation-state declined in importance relative to that of globalization in the production of culture, research and teaching lost their orienting referents.[26] For Readings, the result of this condition is what he observed as the substitution of "excellence"—an abstract notion of quality—for "the historical project of culture," denying the university a unique position within other national enterprises and calling into question how and who should evaluate the work of the university.[27] Readings's trope of "ruin" is particularly apt, in my opinion, because it can refer not only to the status of the *work* of the academic community but also to its physical *place,* the "artificial Antiquity" of the campus itself.[28] The ruins Readings asked us to negotiate are those of the project of modernism as seen through Sigmund Freud's impossible vision of Rome as memory-trace, "in which nothing that has once come into existence will have passed away and all the earlier phases of development continue to exist alongside the latest one."[29] Readings's greatest fear was of a falsely constructed academic community, mired in past repetitions and homogenized to the point of irrelevance. Readings used the image of ruin as an analogy, but with regard to the physical conditions of the campus there are direct referents. Today's campuses are memory-traces of the transformation of higher education and the city in relationship to one another over time. We not only dwell within them, we are compelled to build upon them.

Here the work of the urban scholar Thomas Bender, in extending his early research on the distinction between territorial and networked constructions of community to the contemporary urban university, assists in elaborating possibilities for the university beyond its concerns for self-preservation within an increasingly diffuse landscape for the production of knowledge and the loss of the nation-state as an organizing construct.[30] Dismantling, transforming, or restructuring the cultural canon—a process that recognizes the lack of cohesion in the student body and the skepticism that there is such a thing as a "community of scholars"—is not an issue internal to the campus. It is a reflection of a larger questioning of the idea of community and of contemporary configurations of neighborhood that modernity and modern urbanism obscured:

> Today's cosmopolitanism . . . extends more deeply into the social body. The pluralized culture of the university resembles the complex life of contemporary immigrant neighborhoods. Residents live at once in place-specific urban neighborhoods and in diasporic networks that are not unlike the disciplinary channels that organize academic communications and work across space. Out of this common experience, widely shared in the life of the contemporary metropolis, a worldly humanistic culture well might emerge.[31]

Bender, in borrowing from Readings's analysis of the problematic cultural conditions inside academia, insisted that the way out of them was to look beyond the campus; universities need to refocus on the local (here he meant metropolitan) culture, to participate in partnership with alternative sites for knowledge making, where "the very process of making knowledge is co-terminous with the diffusion of knowledge."[32] Through this local attention, Bender hoped to better situate higher education in engaged, cosmopolitan, and global culture, where "more and more knowledge will be developed outside of universities, in opportunistic and transdisciplinary settings."[33] This recognition of the increasingly nonsituatedness of the academic community builds upon cultural theorist Arjun Appadurai's notions of "imagined worlds," the "scapes" of late-twentieth-century migration and media, which are not only fluid and irregular but also perspectival in construction.[34] Just as immigrant diasporas simultaneously occupy local and global conditions,[35] so too does the academic community. Speaking more directly to the conditions within urban neighborhoods, the sociologist Janet Abu-Lughod stated, "Increasingly, neighborhoods in the central zones of our largest cities no longer fit the old model of 'ethnic enclaves' or 'urban villages.' Many no longer constitute—if indeed they ever did—natural communities where residents share a common culture and pursue a relatively unified set of interests *vis à vis* outsiders."[36] Substitute the word "campus" for "neighborhood" and "academic village" for "urban village"; the campus in this construction can no longer be opposed to its surrounding neighborhood and disconnected from its city.

Mark Taylor's call for new cross-disciplinary and problem-focused programs may begin to address the outmoded structure that defines academia, but his reforms are directed to a "crisis" that is perceived as happening *on* campus.[37] However, what is striking about the recent discourse on the local and global situating of the *academy* is that it often completely ignores the already highly visible situation of the *campus,* where campus greens intersect with city streets in a twenty-four-hour wireless, thoroughly global exchange of knowledge. For even as the online world of degree-granting and credentialing academia grows, so too do place-based institutions (often they are one and the same), responding to a wide variety of internal and external forces. The conclusion I draw from the emerging spaces of Chicago's urban universities, and from the larger national condition of which they are a part, is that the contemporary city is not only the space in which many of Readings's ruined institutions already dwell, but a space that provides the conditions for the community of dissensus that he projected as an alternative to the fictional singular academic community.[38] Not all the lessons to be learned there are positive; nonetheless, just as the nostalgia that produces falsely reconstituted intellectual communities will not solve the problems of higher education, neither will falsely reconstructed ruins of the historical campus or the use of its images of consensus resolve the relationship between city and campus.

While respectful of Readings's commitment to the reform of the university through the building of an internal community of dissensus, I believe that if he had had the opportunity to review his thesis in the twenty-first century, he might have been just as critical of the "university of excellence" but perhaps more willing to look outside the university for models to describe and put into effect his own notions of transdisciplinary negotiation.

The community of dissensus within the university parallels and is increasingly part of life in the city outside it. And it is not safe to ignore these differences by leveling them (the model of midcentury modernism) or pasting them over with nostalgic images (the model of late-twentieth-century postmodernism) in the hopes that this imaginary space can create a consensual community. Further, it is my belief that nostalgically designed campus spaces deny the very real differences within increasingly diverse student bodies, which are revealed by hate-speech issues, affirmative action battles, and identity-oriented conflicts between various student groups.

Instead, I think the sort of space that Readings was after was best described by Iris Marion Young when she stated, "In community persons cease to be other, opaque, not understood, and instead become mutually sympathetic, understanding one another as they understand themselves, fused. Such an ideal of the transparency of subjects to one another denies the difference, or basic asymmetry, of subjects."[39] Instead of "community," which she saw as distinctly antiurban, Young substitutes "urbanity," which she saw as more truly representative of modern and postmodern societies, whether housed in the huge metropolis, the suburb, or large towns:

> I propose to construct a normative ideal of city life as an alternative to both the ideal of community and the liberal individualism it criticizes as asocial. By "city life" I mean a form of social relations which I define as the being together of strangers. In the city persons and groups interact within spaces and institutions they all experience themselves as belonging to, but without those interactions dissolving into unity or commonness.[40]

Young's image of a democratic polity is a complex network of spaces and forums—physical and mediated—through which differences and intersubjectivity are experienced and conflicts are not repressed. But if "in the normative ideal of city life borders are open and undesirable,"[41] the self-contained form of campus, which excludes the city in which it sits, will have to be questioned as well.

I would add, with regard to the life of the campus, that such a concept of urbanity cannot be created solely within the confines of the university's walls. No academic, student, or administrator would make the mistake of choosing to disconnect today's pedagogical techniques and spaces from the global interactions that allow for learning, communication, and shared access to intellectual resources at a great distance; so too is it an error to ignore the opportunities at the periphery of (or sometimes running straight through) the campus. For American universities have always been simultaneously local and global: place-bound, yet containing a depth of global knowledge (within its libraries, research labs, and classrooms) unavailable in practically any other place—*except* the city itself. What is true of the city is also true of the campus; each contains diverse people, cultures, and uses that will always be in conflict over physical spaces, identities, and scarce resources. If we begin to understand the organizing principle of the American campus not as a "landscape" but as a number of fluid, overlapping, and irregular "scapes," the ideal of the semi-isolated academical village and the reality of the fragmented, expanding, and boundaryless urban research university begin to coalesce. This moves the understanding of the modern university beyond the image and the form of a "ruined institution" and suggests ways of organizing its communities in physical spaces that may be within—but may also be outside—its increasingly artificially maintained walls. For a view of the prospects for this campus, take a walk through Chicago's South Loop on a nice spring day (all campuses look best on a nice spring day) or watch a team of students discuss and perhaps build a small community park in the "inner-city." In such spaces the campus is alive and well.

Notes

Introduction

1. In the United States, both "colleges" and "universities" are institutions of higher education. Although the terms are sometimes used interchangeably, in general, colleges only award undergraduate (bachelor's) degrees, whereas universities are research oriented and award both undergraduate and graduate (master's, professional, and Ph.D.) degrees. A number of the institutions cited in this book began as colleges and expanded to become universities; not all changed their names in the process. Often further complicating these designations, many universities are constituted as collections of colleges or professional schools.

2. Bill Readings, *The University in Ruins* (Cambridge, Mass.: Harvard University Press, 1996), 172.

3. Ibid., 19.

4. See, for example, Thomas Bender, "Scholarship, Local Life, and the Necessity of Worldliness," in *The Urban University and Its Identity: Roots, Locations, Roles,* ed. Herman van der Wusten (Boston: Kluwer Academic Publishers, 1998), 17–28.

5. Paul Venable Turner, *Campus: An American Planning Tradition* (Cambridge: MIT Press, 1984), 4.

6. Kurt W. Forster, "From Catechism to Calisthenics: *Cliff Notes* [*sic*] on the History of the American Campus," *Architecture California* 15 (May 1993): 67–68.

7. Thomas Bender, ed., *The University and the City: From Medieval Origins to the Present* (New York: Oxford University Press, 1988), 294.

8. See, for example, Morton White and Lucia White, *The Intellectual versus the City: From Thomas Jefferson to Frank Lloyd Wright* (Cambridge, Mass.: Harvard University Press and MIT Press, 1962). In some, although not all, instances, the Whites interpret a dislike of the state of a city with an antiurban position.

9. Bender, *The University and the City,* v, 3.

10. Turner, *Campus,* 4. Note that Turner is somewhat circumspect on the origin of the term "campus." The *Oxford English Dictionary* gives its origin to Princeton.

11. Bender, *The University and the City,* 290.

12. "Campus: A Place Apart" was the title of an episode of Robert A. M. Stern's *Pride of Place* series on PBS in 1985. See also Robert A. M. Stern, *Pride of Place: Building the American Dream* (Boston: Houghton Mifflin, 1986).

13. Bender, *The University and the City,* 290.

14. Myra Jehlen, *American Incarnation: The Individual, the Nation, and the Continent* (Cambridge, Mass.: Harvard University Press, 1986), 20.

15. Barbara Hadley Stanton, "Cognitive Standards and the Sense of Campus," *Places* 17 (Spring 2005): 38.

16. See, for example, Daniel Bluestone, *Constructing Chicago* (New Haven: Yale University Press, 1991); William Cronon, *Nature's Metropolis: Chicago and the Great West* (New York: W. W. Norton, 1991); and Donald L. Miller, *City of the Century: The Epic of Chicago and the Making of America* (New York: Simon and Schuster, 1996).

17. Carl Smith, *Urban Disorder and the Shape of Belief: The Great Chicago Fire, the Haymarket Bomb, and the Model Town of Pullman* (Chicago: University of Chicago Press, 1995), 4.

18. Ibid., 8.

19. From the film *Chicago Circle Overview: A New Kind of Community* (Chicago: New Student Orientation Committee, in cooperation with the Office of Instructional Resources, UICC, 1965). This film was created to serve as an introduction to the UICC upon the students' move to this newly opened campus.

1. New Institutions for a New Environment

1. J. B. Edmund, *The Magnificent Charter: The Origin and Role of the Morrill Land-Grant Colleges and Universities* (Hicksville, N.Y.: Exposition Press, 1978), xvi.

2. Because states could determine how to allocate their grants, not all land-grant schools were established de novo. Instead, some states applied their funds to enlarge or encourage existing private and public institutions.

3. See, for example, Turner, *Campus*; Richard C. Wade, *The Urban Frontier: Pioneer Life in Early Pittsburgh, Cincinnati, Lexington, Louisville, and St. Louis* (1959; repr., Chicago: University of Chicago Press, 1964); and White and White, *The Intellectual versus the City*.

4. See, for example, "Demography: Chicago as Modern World City," *The Electronic Encyclopedia of Chicago* (2005), www.encyclopedia.chicagohistory.org/pages/962.html (last accessed June 2007); and www.census.gov/history/pdf/History_1890.pdf (last accessed August 2010). Chicago was platted in 1830 and incorporated as a town in 1833, after the Blackhawk War in 1832 ended Native American resistance to settlement.

5. Florence Kelley, "I Go to Work," *Survey Graphic* 67 (June 1, 1927): 274.

6. Frederick Jackson Turner, *The Frontier in American History* (New York: Henry Holt, 1920), 1.

7. Ibid., 2.

8. Ibid., 4. See also Thomas Bender, *Toward an Urban Vision: Ideas and Institutions in Nineteenth-Century America* (Lexington: University Press of Kentucky, 1975).

9. Cronon, *Nature's Metropolis*. In the United States, a city is a legal rather than a physical entity. The U.S. Census Bureau defines the term "urban": "For Census 2000, the Census Bureau classifies as 'urban' all territory, population, and housing units located within an urbanized area (UA) or an urban cluster (UC). It delineates UA and UC boundaries to encompass densely settled territory." www.census.gov/geo/www/ua/ua_2k.html (last accessed August 2010). The definition of "densely settled" changes from census to census.

10. Turner, *The Frontier in American History*, 3.

11. Annette Kolodny, "Letting Go Our Grand Obsessions: Notes toward a New Literary History of the American Frontiers," in *Subjects and Citizens: Nation, Race, and Gender from Oroonoko to Anita Hill,* ed. Michael Moon and Cathy N. Davidson (Durham, N.C.: Duke University Press, 1995), 11. See also Neil Smith, *The New Urban Frontier: Gentrification and the Revanchist City* (New York: Routledge, 1996).

12. Benedict Anderson, *Imagined Communities: Reflections on the Origin and Spread of Nationalism,* rev. ed. (New York: Verso, 1991), 145.

13. Smith, *Urban Disorder and the Shape of Belief,* 1.

14. Thomas Lee Philpott, *The Slum and the Ghetto: Neighborhood Deterioration and Middle-Class Reform, Chicago, 1880–1930* (New York: Oxford University Press, 1978), 13.

15. Ibid., 3, 7.

16. Charles J. Hull, *Reflections from a Busy Life* (Chicago: Knight and Leonard, Printers, 1881), 42, 83. Hull's wife died in 1869, his son in 1866, and his daughter in 1874. The Hulls were no longer living at the house when the Chicago Fire broke out nearby in 1871. Hull's memoir was written in the same year that he willed his estate to his cousin Helen Culver, who had come to live with the family as his wife was dying. Hull died in 1889.

17. Peggy Glowacki, "Helen Culver," in *Women Building Chicago, 1790–1990: A Biographical Dictionary,* ed. Rima Lunin Schultz and Adele Hast (Bloomington and Indianapolis: Indiana University Press, 2001), 202–205. See also Thomas W. Goodspeed, "Helen Culver," *University [of Chicago] Record* 9 (January 1923).

18. Allen B. Pond, "The Settlement House III," *Brickbuilder* 11 (September 1902): 178.

19. Sharon Haar, "At Home in Public," in *Embodied Utopias: Gender, Social Change, and the Modern Metropolis,* ed. Amy Bingaman, Lise Sanders, and Rebecca Zorach (New York: Routledge, 2002), 99–115.

20. Jehlen, *American Incarnation,* 3.

21. *Oxford English Dictionary,* online edition, www.oed.com/.

22. Jane Addams, "The Objective Value of a Social Settlement" and "The Subjective Necessity for Social Settlements," in *Philanthropy and Social Progress* (1893; repr., College Park, Md.: McGrath, 1969).

23. Addams, "The Objective Value of a Social Settlement," 33, 30.

24. Dolores Hayden, *The Grand Domestic Revolution: A History of Feminist Designs for American Homes, Neighborhoods, and Cities* (Cambridge: MIT Press, 1981), 174.

25. Horace Bushnell, "The Age of Homespun" (1851), quoted in Bender, *Toward an Urban Vision,* 53. Numerous narratives of this mid-nineteenth-century process exist, each cast in a different conceptual frame. A few include Richard Hofstadter, *The Age of Reform: From Bryan to FDR* (1955; repr., New York: Alfred A. Knopf, 1968); John H. Ehrenreich, *The Altruistic Imagination: A History of Social Work and Social Policy in the United States* (Ithaca, N.Y.: Cornell University Press, 1985); Carol Smith-Rosenberg, *Disorderly Conduct: Visions of Gender in Victorian America* (New York: Oxford University Press, 1985).

26. Jane Addams, *Twenty Years at Hull-House* (1910; repr., New York: Penguin Books, 1981), 89.

27. Smith-Rosenberg, *Disorderly Conduct*, 20.

28. Hannah Arendt, *The Human Condition* (Chicago: University of Chicago Press, 1958), 27–28.

29. Hayden, *The Grand Domestic Revolution*, 174.

30. Addams, "The Subjective Necessity for Social Settlements," 6, 22–26.

31. Rebecca Louise Sherrick, "Private Visions, Public Lives: The Hull-House Women in the Progressive Era" (Ph.D. diss., Northwestern University, 1980), 6. See also Gwendolyn Wright, *Moralism and the Model Home: Domestic Architecture and Cultural Conflict in Chicago, 1873–1913* (Chicago: University of Chicago Press, 1980), 107. More recently scholars have criticized Addams and other women of her time for obscuring their own autobiographies in their narrations of the work of the collectivity. Space does not allow for a detailed analysis of this critique here. Suffice it to say that Hull-House residents focused on a more extensive study and public scrutiny of the details of tenement life than they would have allowed in their own homes. "Working on the borders between their own white middle-class Protestant culture and the diverse cultures of their neighbors, they frequently experienced the best of both worlds, enjoying the superiority conferred by their cultural identity yet benefiting as well from the cultural values their neighbors assigned to their work." Kathryn Kish Sklar, *Florence Kelley and the Nation's Work: The Rise of Women's Political Culture, 1830–1900* (New Haven: Yale University Press, 1995), 196.

32. White and White, *The Intellectual versus the City*. They similarly argue that Pragmatic philosophers—such as John Dewey—and Chicago school sociologists were antiurban.

33. Shannon Jackson, "Civic Play-Housekeeping: Gender, Theatre, and American Reform," *Theatre Journal* 48 (1996): 339.

34. Michel de Certeau, *The Practice of Everyday Life,* trans. Steven Rendell (Berkeley and Los Angeles: University of California Press, 1984); originally published as *L'Invention du quotidien* (1980).

35. I would like to thank Mary Ann Johnson, formerly director of the Jane Addams Memorial Hull-House Museum, for assistance with this information. Vincent L. Michael provides the most detailed account of the sequence of building projects for Hull-House in "Recovering the Layout of the Hull House Complex," tigger.uic.edu/htbin/cgiwrap/bin/urbanexp/main.cgi?file=new/show_doc.ptt&doc=834&chap=32 (last accessed August 2010). The narrative (constructed from letters, journal and newspaper articles, building permits, and other materials in the Jane Addams Memorial Collection and Hull-House Association Records at UIC) illustrates the complexity of this enterprise. It also illuminates how the various activities of the settlement moved around the complex as new buildings were added and needs changed. For an analysis of how public and private activities were distributed around the settlement, see my *Urban Archaeology Chicago: The Hull-House Settlement and the University of Illinois at Chicago,* www.arch.uic.edu/urbanarch (last accessed August 2010).

36. Pond, "The Settlement House III," 183.

37. James Weber Linn, *Jane Addams: A Biography* (New York: D. Appleton-Century, 1935), 209.

38. Guy Szuberla, "Three Chicago Settlements: Their Architectural Form and Social Meaning," *Journal of the Illinois Historical Society* 70 (May 1977): 116.

39. Addams, *Twenty Years at Hull-House,* 114.

40. Florence Kelley, "Hull House," *New England Magazine* 18 (July 1898): 552.

41. See, for example, Hull-House's *Weekly Programmes* of the early 1890s, Hull-House Association Records, Special Collections, University of Illinois at Chicago.

42. Helen Lefkowitz-Horowitz, "Hull-House as Women's Space," *Chicago History* 12 (Winter 1983–1984): 55.

43. Additionally, many who engaged in Hull-House activities were never residents. The building within the settlement that most resembled a women's dormitory as described by Lefkowitz-Horowitz was the Jane Club, which housed young, single, working women.

44. Allen F. Davis, *Spearheads for Reform: The Social Settlement and the Progressive Movement: 1890–1914* (New York: Oxford University Press, 1967), 40.

45. Ibid., 43.

46. Vincent L. Michael has worked through the most accurate dating of the Hull-House complex construction. Michael, "Evolution of Hull House," www.uic.edu/jaddams/hull/urbanexp/geography/groundplans.htm# (last accessed August 2009).

47. Charles Goodspeed to William Rainey Harper, quoted in NBBJ [Architectural Consultant Team], *The University of Chicago Campus Master Plan* ([Chicago?], 1999), 2.

48. Ibid.

49. Steven J. Diner, *A City and Its Universities: Public Policy in Chicago, 1892–1919* (Chapel Hill: University of North Carolina Press, 1980), 13.

50. John R. Thelin, *A History of American Higher Education* (Baltimore: The Johns Hopkins University Press, 2004), 112.

51. Ibid., 115.

52. A. D. F. Hamlin, "Recent American College Architecture," in *Portraits of the American University: 1890–1910*, ed. James C. Stone and Donald P. DeNevi (San Francisco: Jossey-Bass, 1971), 362.

53. Paul Venable Turner, *Campus,* 175–177.

54. Hamlin, "Recent American College Architecture," 364.

55. Between World Wars I and II, enrollment in higher education grew five times, signaling a shift toward mass higher education. Thelin, *A History of American Higher Education,* 205.

2. City as Laboratory

1. Catherine Peaden, "Jane Addams and the Social Rhetoric of Democracy," in *Oratorical Culture in Nineteenth-Century America: Transformations in the Theory and*

Practice of Rhetoric, ed. Gregory Clark and S. Michael Halloran (Carbondale: Southern Illinois University Press, 1993), 184.

2. Gregory Clark and S. Michael Halloran, "Transformations of Public Discourse in Nineteenth-Century America," in Clark and Halloran, *Oratorical Culture in Nineteenth-Century America,* 5–6. See also Stanley Fish, "Rhetoric" (1990), in *The Stanley Fish Reader,* ed. H. Aram Veeser (Cambridge, Mass.: Blackwell, 1999).

3. Addams, *Twenty Years at Hull-House,* 294.

4. Florence Kelley in *Century Magazine,* February 1907, quoted in a brochure for the Practical Housekeeping Center, 1909, Hull-House Association Records, Special Collections, University of Illinois at Chicago.

5. Practical Housekeeping Center, brochure dated 1909, Hull-House Association Records, Special Collections, University of Illinois at Chicago.

6. Richard Wade, introduction to Philpott, *The Slum and the Ghetto,* xv.

7. There is some speculation on the part of Guy Szuberla and Helen Lefkowitz-Horowitz that the tenement itself was never built because of Addams's objection to single working mothers. But my research has not revealed any controversy to this effect. It is possible that the tenement proposal was Pond's and not part of the intention of the donors of the building.

8. Addams, *Twenty Years at Hull-House,* 183.

9. James L. Machor, *Pastoral Cities: Urban Ideals, and the Symbolic Landscape of America* (Madison: University of Wisconsin Press, 1987), 153.

10. See, for example, Louis Menand, *The Metaphysical Club: A Story of Ideas in America* (New York: Farrar, Straus, and Giroux, 2001).

11. John Dewey, "The School as Social Center," in *National Education Association Proceedings* (Chicago: University of Chicago Press, 1902), 373.

12. Ibid., 31.

13. Daniel H. Burnham and Edward H. Bennett, "Metropolis of the Midwest," in *Plan of Chicago* (1909; repr., New York: Princeton Architectural Press, 1993), 1.

14. Kristen Schaffer, "Fabric of City Life: The Social Agenda in Burnham's Draft of the *Plan of Chicago,*" new introduction to Burnham and Bennett, *Plan of Chicago,* viii.

15. Schaffer, "Fabric of City Life," xiii.

16. Rivka Shpak Lissak, *Pluralism and Progressives: Hull House and the New Immigrants, 1890–1919* (Chicago: University of Chicago Press, 1989), 15, 6.

17. Residents of Hull-House, *Hull-House Maps and Papers* (1895; repr., New York: Arno Press, 1970). In addition to the maps and commentary on them, the collection also included chapters on labor, art, immigrant groups, and charity work.

18. Agnes S. Holbrook, "Map Notes and Comments," in Residents of Hull-House, *Hull-House Maps and Papers,* 11.

19. Ibid., 13.

20. Ibid., 14.

21. Kathryn Kish Sklar, "Hull House in the 1890s: A Community of Women Reformers," *Signs* 10 (Summer 1985): 677.

22. James Clifford, *The Predicament of Culture: Twentieth-Century Ethnography, Literature, and Art* (Cambridge, Mass.: Harvard University Press, 1988), 41.

23. Kathryn Kish Sklar, "*Hull-House Maps and Papers*: Social Science as Women's Work in the 1890s," in *The Social Survey Movement in Historical Perspective, 1880–1940,* ed. Martin Bulmer, Kevin Bales, and Kathryn Kish Sklar (New York: Cambridge University Press, 1991), 139.

24. Sklar, *Florence Kelley and the Nation's Work,* 222.

25. Ibid., 193.

26. Addams, "Prefatory Notes," in Residents of Hull-House, *Hull-House Maps and Papers,* vii–viii. *The Jane Addams Papers,* microfilm edition (Ann Arbor, Mich.: University Microfilms International, 1984), contain twenty-three investigations conducted by Hull-House residents between the years 1892 and 1933.

27. Sklar, "*Hull-House Maps and Papers,*" 115.

28. Laurence E. Veysey, *The Emergence of the American University* (Chicago: University of Chicago Press, 1965), 175. Almost all subsequent studies of higher education in the United States cite Veysey as an important source.

29. Roger L. Geiger, *To Advance Knowledge: The Growth of American Research Universities, 1900–1940* (New York: Oxford University Press, 1986), 1.

30. Ibid., 4.

31. Thelin, *A History of American Higher Education,* 135.

32. Veysey, *The Emergence of the American University,* 142.

33. Diner, *A City and Its Universities,* 19. Harper's "Decennial Report" to the university's board of trustees outlined his understanding of how the university was built in its first decade. He acknowledged its strength in the arts, literature, and science over "technology" and suggested that professional schools would be the next phase of growth. He also described how the university was divided into departments with the goal of both managing administration and developing independent areas of expertise. William Rainey Harper, "Decennial Report" (1902), in *American Higher Education: A Documentary History,* ed. Richard Hofstadter and Wilson Smith (Chicago: University of Chicago Press, 1961), 773–84.

34. Burton Bledstein, *The Culture of Professionalism: The Middle Class and the Development of Higher Education in America* (New York: W. W. Norton, 1976), 326.

35. Diner, *A City and Its Universities,* 9.

36. Ibid., 45.

37. Edith Abbott, *The Tenements of Chicago, 1908–1935* (1936; repr., New York: Arno Press, 1970).

38. Ernest W. Burgess, "A Short History of Urban Research at the University of Chicago before 1946," in *Urban Sociology,* ed. Ernest W. Burgess and Donald J. Bogue, abr. ed. (Chicago: University of Chicago Press, 1967), 4.

39. See Mary Jo Deegan, *Jane Addams and the Men of the Chicago School, 1892–1918* (New Brunswick, N.J.: Transaction Books, 1988).

40. Ernest W. Burgess, "The Social Survey: A Field for Constructive Service by Departments of Sociology," in *The Basic Writings of Ernest W. Burgess,* ed. Donald J. Bogue (1916; repr., Chicago: Community and Family Study Center, The University of Chicago, 1974), 14.

41. Robert E. Park, "The City: Suggestions for the Investigation of Human

Behavior in the Urban Environment," in *The City: Suggestions for the Investigation of Human Behavior in the Urban Environment,* ed. Robert E. Park, Ernest W. Burgess, and Roderick D. McKenzie (1925; repr., Chicago: University of Chicago Press, 1967), 8, 46.

42. Sudhir Venkatesh, "Chicago's Pragmatic Planners: American Sociology and the Myth of Community," *Social Science History* 25 (Summer 2001): 282.

43. Ernest W. Burgess, "Can Neighborhood Work Have a Scientific Basis?" in Park, Burgess, and McKenzie, *The City,* 143.

44. Ernest W. Burgess, "The Growth of the City: An Introduction to a Research Project," in Park, Burgess, and McKenzie, *The City,* 53.

45. "An Encroaching Menace," *Life,* April 11, 1955, 125.

46. Lawrence Veiller, "Slum Clearance," *Proceedings of the Tenth National Conference on Housing,* January 1929, quoted in M. Christine Boyer, *Dreaming the Rational City: The Myth of American City Planning* (Cambridge: MIT Press, 1983), 233.

47. For a discussion of some of the subjective interests underlying the work of the early Chicago school sociologists, see Venkatesh, "Chicago's Pragmatic Planners."

3. *Modern City, Modern Campus*

1. Studs Terkel, *Division Street: America* (1967; repr., New York: New Press, 1993), 261. Terkel wrote that *Division Street* became the prologue to *Race: How Blacks and Whites Think and Feel about the American Obsession* (1992). The interviewees in *Division Street* often used abstract ideas of urban change as codes for racial succession.

2. Maurice R. Berube, *The Urban University in America* (Westport, Conn.: Greenwood Press, 1978), 46; "Higher Education for Urban America: Report of a National Conference of Educators, Public Officials, and Other Civic Leaders," special supplement, *Educational Record* 46 (1965).

3. David Boroff, "The Case for 'The Asphalt Campus,'" *New York Times Magazine,* April 21, 1963, 83.

4. J. Martin Klotsche, *The Urban University and the Future of Our Cities* (New York: Harper and Row, 1966), 50–52.

5. Ibid., 29.

6. Frederick O'R. Hayes, symposium discussant, in "The Role of the University in Urban America," in "Higher Education for Urban America," 325.

7. Richard Sennett and Jonathan Cobb, *The Hidden Injuries of Class* (New York: W. W. Norton, 1972).

8. Ibid., 11–16.

9. Ibid., 17; Gerald D. Suttles, *The Social Order of the Slum: Ethnicity and Territory in the Inner City* (Chicago: University of Chicago Press, 1968). Thomas Lee Philpott showed that different dynamics were at work in communities defined by race. Philpott, *The Slum and the Ghetto.*

10. Sennett and Cobb, *The Hidden Injuries of Class,* 179. Urban sociologist Herbert Gans, who is well known for living in the communities he studied, also noted an antipathy to higher education in inner-city ethnic communities. Gans, *The Urban*

Villagers: Group and Class in the Life of Italian-Americans (New York: Free Press, 1962). The epilogue to Gans's book was crafted as an analysis and critique of urban renewal and displacement as it affected inner-city, ethnically white neighborhoods.

11. Chicago and its immediate environs are host to a large number of colleges and universities. IIT, UICC, and the University of Chicago are chosen for discussion because of the way they exemplify key examples of urban and campus design dynamics in the middle of the twentieth century.

12. Chicago was one of the cities to begin to build public housing as an alternative to slum tenement housing before the era of large-scale public housing, codified in the Federal Housing Act of 1949, got underway. Mayor Martin Kennelly (1947–1955) initiated plans for new highways prior to the National Interstate and Defense Highways Act of 1956 (Federal-Aid Highway Act of 1956) in order, among other things, to shore up the strength of the Loop, the city's central business district.

13. Arnold R. Hirsch, *Making the Second Ghetto: Race and Housing in Chicago, 1940–1960* (1983; repr., Chicago: University of Chicago Press, 1998); St. Clair Drake and Horace R. Cayton, *Black Metropolis: A Study of Negro Life in a Northern City,* rev. ed. (Chicago: University of Chicago Press, 1993 [first edition published 1945]); Wim de Wit, "The Rise of Public Housing in Chicago, 1930–1960," in *Chicago Architecture and Design, 1923–1993: Reconfiguration of an American Metropolis,* ed. John Zukowsky (Chicago: Art Institute of Chicago, 1993), 233–245.

14. Adam Cohen and Elizabeth Taylor, *American Pharaoh: Mayor Richard J. Daley. His Battle for Chicago and the Nation* (New York: Little, Brown, 2000), 224–233.

15. Under the Kennelly administration in the early 1950s, plans were proposed to build a campus on the north side of the main stem of the Chicago River. The "Fort Dearborn Project" included residential development; new city, county, state, and federal buildings; and the proposed campus. It was designed by the architectural firm Skidmore, Owings & Merrill (SOM).

16. Chicago Department of City Planning, *Development Plan for the Central Area of Chicago, August 1958,* Ira J. Bach, Commissioner, 21. For general reception of the CAC program in the press, see, for example, Ruth Moore, "Renewal Program Gets Daley Boost," *Chicago Sun-Times,* August 23, 1958.

17. Chicago Department of City Planning, *Development Plan for the Central Area of Chicago,* 29, 31.

18. Larry Bennett, "Postwar Redevelopment in Chicago: The Declining Politics of Party and the Rise of Neighborhood Politics," in *Unequal Partnerships: The Political Economy of Urban Redevelopment in Postwar America,* ed. Gregory D. Squires (New Brunswick, N.J.: Rutgers University Press, 1989), 167–171.

19. Phyllis Lambert, "Learning a Language," in *Mies in America,* ed. Phyllis Lambert (New York: Harry N. Abrams, 2001), 224.

20. Sarah Whiting, "Bas Relief Urbanism: Chicago's Figured Field," in Lambert, *Mies in America,* 649.

21. Ibid., 656. The history of the design and building of IIT is an important part of American modern urban design and planning, too complex to detail here. Much of the story and its mythology are clarified in the recent writing of Lambert and Whiting.

22. Ibid., 676.

23. Lambert, "Learning a Language," 234.

24. Ibid., 273, 275.

25. Sarah Whiting, "Super!" *Log* 16 (Spring/Summer 2009): 22.

26. NBBJ, *The University of Chicago Campus Master Plan*, 4.

27. Henry S. Webber, "The University of Chicago and Its Neighbors," in *The University as Urban Developer: Case Studies and Analysis,* ed. David C. Perry and Wim Wiewel (Armonk, N.Y.: M. E. Sharpe, 2005), 69.

28. Eero Saarinen, "Campus Planning: The Unique World of the University," *Architectural Record* 128 (November 1960): 123–130.

29. "Rapid Progress in Hyde Park–Kenwood," *Architectural Record* 128 (November 1960): 140.

30. Several of the documents related to 1950s urban renewal can be found at the HPKCC page "The Early Alternative Plans for Urban Renewal: Overall, Projects, and UC Campus," http://www.hydepark.org/historicpres/urbanrenaltern.htm (last accessed August 2009).

31. "The Re-making of South-East Chicago," *Architectural Record* 128 (November 1960): 131–139.

32. Jane Jacobs, *The Death and Life of Great American Cities* (New York: Vintage Books, 1961), 44–45. There have been extensive studies of the University of Chicago and its relationship to urban renewal in Hyde Park, Kenwood, and, slightly later, Woodlawn, which Webber noted has served as a negative example of mid-century urban planning and design. Webber, "The University of Chicago and Its Neighbors." See for example, Hirsch, *Making the Second Ghetto*; Peter H. Rossi and Robert Dentler, *The Politics of Urban Renewal: The Chicago Findings* (New York: Free Press, 1961).

33. Arnold Hirsch noted, "The University of Chicago's urban renewal plans, however, were not foisted on an unwilling citizenry." *Making the Second Ghetto,* 139. More recently, Amanda Seligman detailed the response of community organizations to racial succession in Chicago's West Side neighborhoods. Amanda I. Seligman, *Block by Block: Neighborhoods and Public Policy on Chicago's West Side* (Chicago: University of Chicago Press, 2005). The Chicago Community Inventory was established in 1946 and the Community and Family Study Center in 1961 to continue the work of older urban studies programs. See Burgess and Bogue, *Urban Sociology*; and Otis Dudley and Beverly Duncan, *The Negro Population of Chicago: A Study of Residential Succession,* Monograph Series of the Chicago Community Inventory of the University of Chicago (Chicago: University of Chicago Press, 1957).

34. Daniel Bluestone, "Preservation and Renewal in Post–World War II Chicago," *Journal of Architectural Education* 47 (May 1994): 214.

35. Julian Levi, "Slum Fighter Levi Tells What to Do," *Life,* April 11, 1955, 134; "An Encroaching Menace," *Life,* April 11, 1955, 125–134. Levi concluded his remarks saying, "If you bring all your community's dwelling and services up to standard, you begin to guarantee its preservation. To restore such standards in Hyde Park we will have to tear down whole blocks of buildings which are infecting their environs. Two

years ago our people wondered if the job could be done. Today the question is not whether it can be done but how soon we can put the bold finishing touch on it—so all I hear is 'When will the first building come down?'" (134). *Newsweek* also highlighted Chicago's renewal, particularly with regard to the growth of postwar business and its readiness to resolve urban problems, in "The New Chicago," *Newsweek*, August 16, 1954, 31–36. Hirsch offered a compelling discussion of the relationship among the SECC, HPKCC, and the University of Chicago. Hirsch, *Making the Second Ghetto*, 135–170.

36. Julian H. Levi, "The Influence of Environment on Urban Institutions," *Educational Record* 52 (April 1961): 137. See also Levi, "Private Property Rights vs. Public Purpose of Renewal: Handle with Care," *Journal of Housing* 17 (April 1960): 142–145.

37. Fred M. Hechinger, "Campus vs. Slums: Urban Universities Join Battle for Neighborhood Renewal," *New York Times*, October 1, 1961.

38. Lawrence A. Kimpton, quoted in "Rapid Progress in Hyde Park–Kenwood," 141.

39. Hechinger, "Campus vs. Slums."

40. *Housing Act of 1959*, Public Law 86-372, September 23, 1959, *U.S. Statutes at Large*, 73 (1959) (GPO, 1960), 677.

41. "Urban Renewal Act a Boon to Chicago," *Chicago Sun-Times*, April 1, 1960.

42. Philip Hauser, quoted in "Rapid Progress in Hyde Park–Kenwood," 141.

43. David B. Carlson, "Town and Gown," *Architectural Forum* 118 (March 1963): 92.

44. Ibid. See also Leonard Buder, "Colleges Clear Out Slums to Extend City Campuses," *New York Times*, January 13, 1965; and "Higher Education for Urban America."

45. *Chicago Circle Overview*.

4. Classrooms off the Expressway

1. In the *Community Areas Map* created by the University of Chicago sociologists in the late 1920s, the Near West Side is bounded by the South Branch of the Chicago River to the east, Sixteenth Street to the south, and railroad tracks to the north and west. The new highways and later the University of Illinois campus would significantly change the geography of "Area 28," although not its official boundaries.

2. Chicago journalist and Daley biographer Mike Royko provided an image of these two cities in his book *Boss*, narrating a journey with Daley from his home in the Bridgeport neighborhood to City Hall in the Loop. As they travel along the new Dan Ryan and Kennedy expressways, they pass entrances to the new Stevenson and Eisenhower expressways, vast quantities of high-rise public housing, and UICC, all of which Daley played a significant role in building. They also pass by the slums of the Black Belt and the Puerto Rican neighborhoods, which Daley's policies had a role in maintaining. Royko, *Boss: Richard J. Daley of Chicago* (New York: Penguin Books, 1971), 11–12. A more recent assessment of Daley stresses the relationship between the development of his political career and that of the city and segregation. See Cohen and Taylor, *American Pharaoh*.

3. "The Scope and Mission of the University and the Basic Planning Assumptions of Its Campuses," faculty letter from the Office of the President, University of Illinois, no. 231, July 10, 1972, University Archives, University of Illinois at Chicago.

4. Norman A. Parker, "Mission Statement" (undated [1965?]); University Archives, University of Illinois at Chicago.

5. "Undergraduate Division of the University of Illinois in Chicago, Program, Administration, and Policies," August 13, 1946, University Archives, University of Illinois at Chicago.

6. The chronology of the steps taken by the faculty and administration of Navy Pier, the faculty and administration of UIUC, the trustees of the University of Illinois, the Illinois Board of Higher Education, and the state legislature is too lengthy for the specific concerns of this book. Numerous efforts, some in series and others in parallel, were made to address and give definition to the needs of the Chicago branch.

7. E. L. Stouffer, "Proposed Permanent Undergraduate College—Chicago," December 28, 1953; E. L. Stouffer to C. S. Havens, "Memo: Undergraduate Campus—Chicago," February 2, 1954; Richard Lawrence Nelson to James V. Edsall, April 19, 1954; H. W. Pearce, "Campus Planning Principles Chicago Undergraduate Division," May 24, 1956; all in University Archives, University of Illinois at Chicago.

8. "U of I Pledges a Study of Fort Dearborn Project," *Chicago Daily Tribune,* March 20, 1954. Several private universities suggested to the state commission studying the need for the new campus that it should "consider giving tax support to private universities, rather than build a completely new institution" (ibid.).

9. As Gerald D. Suttles designated it in *The Social Order of the Slum.*

10. See Real Estate Research Corporation (RERC) with the assistance of Skidmore, Owings & Merrill, Naess & Murphy, Sargent & Lundy, "Analysis of Sites for the Campus of the Chicago Undergraduate Division, University of Illinois," reports dated 1954, [1955?], and October 1958; all in University Archives, University of Illinois at Chicago.

11. The issues around the siting of the campus are summarized in Paul Venable Turner, *Campus.* They are discussed at length in George Rosen, *Decision-Making Chicago Style: The Genesis of a University of Illinois Campus* (Chicago: University of Illinois Press, 1980). Rosen's book provides considerable material on the history leading to the location of the campus (although not on its design) and analyzes the material from the position of "a theory of public-policy decision-making" (7) rather than of the spatial politics of urban planning and design. The plans for the UICC campus are discussed in detail in the publication Educational Facilities Laboratories, Inc. (EFL), *Bricks and Mortarboards: A Report on College Planning and Building* (New York: Ford Foundation, undated [1964?]).

12. Subcommittee on Physical Planning for the Chicago Undergraduate Division, "Report on Low, Medium, and High Rise Buildings," December 16, 1954, University Archives, University of Illinois at Chicago.

13. Thus, one of the first sites they considered, Miller-Meadows, was situated in

a forest preserve. The litigation that would have been required to transfer title to that land eventually appeared too onerous. The trustees then turned for their first choice to a suburban golf course located in Riverside, a nonurban site that met the criteria for commuter access.

14. While the site-selection process was covered by the major Chicago newspapers, the local community papers, such as the *North Riverside Star,* the *Riverside News,* the *Austin News,* and the *Garfieldian,* closely monitored and advocated for their communities' positions on the location of the campus.

15. This is a summary of the issues as they were played out at the time. Rosen's *Decision-Making Chicago Style* provides the background for some of the discussion in this section, but my text is drawn from a careful reading of the decision as it was covered in the local and city press and of materials that have come to light since his book was written.

16. Amanda Seligman offers a compelling narrative of neighborhood positions and actions in *Block by Block,* 99–118.

17. RERC, "Analysis of Sites," October 1958, 5–6.

18. Ibid., 4.

19. Ibid., 5.

20. See, for example, Norman A. Parker and James Edsell, "A Ten-Year Building Space and Land Estimate for Development of a General Campus Plan," distributed February 8, 1960, University Archives, University of Illinois at Chicago. Even at this late date, the exact program of the new university was not developed.

21. RERC, "Analysis of Sites," 31.

22. Walter Netsch, interview by Fred Beuttler and Robert Remini, August 4, 1998, Office of the UIC Historian, University of Illinois at Chicago.

23. Rosen, *Decision-Making Chicago Style,* 73. Based on interviews, Rosen stated that Phil Doyle, executive director of the CLCC, suggested the site in early 1959 and that it came up again "at the end of that year during a trip made to Washington by the mayor and his urban advisers." This is conceivable, although it would not have been until after November 1959 that the site would appear to be legally viable. The RERC had not previously considered any CLCC sites.

24. Barbara Ferman, quoted in Rachel Webber, Nik Theodore, and Charles Hoch, "Private Choices and Public Obligations: The Ethics of University Real Estate Development," in Perry and Wiewel, *The University as Urban Developer,* 292.

25. I disagree with Webber, Theodore, and Hoch's claim that the federal government allowed Daley to use the Harrison–Halsted site for the university as a quid pro quo for his support for John F. Kennedy's election as president, which is not to say that Daley's overall plans for Chicago renewal did not benefit from his role in national politics. Webber, Theodore, and Hoch, "Private Choices and Public Obligations," 292.

26. Hull-House Association Board of Trustees, Minutes, April 28, 1960, Hull-House Association Board of Trustees Papers, Special Collections, University of Illinois at Chicago. A May 11, 1960, *Daily News* article discussing local settlement workers' opposition to the Garfield Park plan stated, "Ira J. Bach, city plan commissioner,

said he has ordered a restudy of 25 locations originally suggested for the campus in the event that neither Garfield Park nor the south of the Loop site is available." Although the article did not discuss the Harrison–Halsted site, it was presented in a plan. "Nuns Oppose U.I. Plan," *Daily News,* May 11, 1960.

27. Agenda for meetings, June 9, 1960, University of Illinois—Chicago Campus, 6, University Archives, University of Illinois at Chicago.

28. Criteria for Evaluation of Harrison–Halsted Site, December 7, 1960; agenda for December 28, 1960, meeting, University of Illinois Chicago Undergraduate Division; both in University Archives, University of Illinois at Chicago.

29. Ruth Moore, "Odds Favor U. of I. Site on West Side," *Chicago Sun-Times,* July 6, 1960.

30. Hull-House Association Board of Trustees, Minutes, September 29, 1960, Hull-House Association Board of Trustees Papers, Special Collections, University of Illinois at Chicago.

31. West Central Association, *Bulletin,* November 1960, Hull-House Association Board of Trustees Papers, Special Collections, University of Illinois at Chicago.

32. CLCC, "Revision No. 1 to the Redevelopment Plan for Slum and Blighted Area Redevelopment Project Harrison–Halsted," March 28, 1961, Municipal Reference Library, Harold Washington Library Center, Chicago; Ira J. Bach, "Report to the Chicago Plan Commission: Proposed Designation of Redevelopment Project Areas and Proposed Redevelopment Plans for Development of Chicago Campus of University of Illinois and Adjacent Residential Areas," April 6, 1961, Hull-House Association Board of Trustees Papers, Special Collections, University of Illinois at Chicago.

33. Florence Scala, interview by Robert Remini and Fred Beuttler, June 26, 1998, Office of the UIC Historian, University of Illinois at Chicago. In retrospect Scala noted the change in composition of the board of trustees and their conflicting interests.

34. Sudhir Venkatesh described changes to the understanding of Chicago as a "city of neighborhoods" in the postwar period. Venkatesh, "Chicago's Pragmatic Planners," 296–297.

35. For the most detailed accounts of Hull-House after Jane Addams's death, see Mary Lynn McCree Bryan and Allen F. Davis, *100 Years at Hull-House* (Bloomington: Indiana University Press, 1990); and *Urban Experience in Chicago: Hull-House and Its Neighborhoods 1889–1963,* http://www.uic.edu/jaddams/hull/urbanexp (last accessed November 2007).

36. Anton Vleek, "Hull House" (1948), 18–19, Hull-House Association Board of Trustees Papers, Special Collections, University of Illinois at Chicago.

37. [Space Utilization] Scheme D-1, September 1959, "Hull House," August 8, 1958, Hull-House Association Board of Trustees Papers, Special Collections, University of Illinois at Chicago.

38. Janet P. Murray, "Long Range Plans: A Study of Present Program with Special Attention to the Future," November 1, 1959, 2, Hull-House Association Board of Trustees Papers, Special Collections, University of Illinois at Chicago.

39. Ibid., 3.

40. Ibid., 21, 26–28.

41. Ibid., 28.

42. Jean Reynolds, "Continuation of February 20, 1961, Proposal for Hull-House Neighborhood Social Work Center," February 24, 1961, 29, 30, Hull-House Association Board of Trustees Papers, Special Collections, University of Illinois at Chicago.

43. "The Future of Hull-House: Proceedings of a Board Meeting," *Social Science Review* 36 (June 1962): 125. The symposium to discuss the future of the Hull-House Association, in light of the changing conditions in its neighborhood, took place in June 1961. The meeting went beyond the discussion of what to do with the buildings to address the role of the social settlement in changing urban and global environments.

44. Rosen, *Decision-Making Chicago Style,* 103–108.

45. Georgie Anne Geyer, "The Heritage of Jane Addams: Florence Scala Fills the Void," *Chicago Scene* (January 1964): 22–27. See also Bruce Cook, "Florence Scala's Fight: Renewal without Representation," *U.S. Catholic* 30 (July 1964): 20–25.

46. Florence Scala, interview by Robert Remini and Fred Beuttler, July 30, 1998, Office of the UIC Historian, University of Illinois at Chicago. In the early 1950s, Scala kept a careful photographic record of deteriorated buildings in the Harrison–Halsted area and conveyed information about them to the Building Department; the back of each photograph records various actions taken with regard to each property; the photographs are now held by the Office of the UIC Historian, University of Illinois at Chicago. Some buildings were eventually razed, creating more empty lots in the neighborhood.

47. CLCC, "Land Use Plan, Exhibit No. 1," "Slum and Blighted Area Redevelopment Project Harrison–Halsted," January 10, 1958, Municipal Reference Library, Harold Washington Library Center; CLCC, "Harrison–Halsted Project Proposed Plan—Ultimate," July 18, 1956, Hull-House Association Board of Trustees Papers, Special Collections, University of Illinois at Chicago.

48. HHCPP, "Our Neighbors and Urban Renewal Progress Report, September 1956–1957," n.d., Hull-House Association Board of Trustees Papers, Special Collections, University of Illinois at Chicago. The split between Hull-House and the NWSPB was caused in part by disagreements over the allocation of funds, visions for the neighborhood, and local political issues; see Rosen, *Decision-Making Chicago Style.*

49. HHCPP, "Observations and Future Possibilities in the Hull House Area," February 4, 1959; Alvin H. Eichholz, "Community Organization in Urban Renewal: Near West Side Problems" (October 1959); HHCPP, Minutes, September 24, 1958; all in Hull-House Association Board of Trustees Papers, Special Collections, University of Illinois at Chicago.

50. Hull-House Association Board of Trustees, Minutes, March 25, 1960, Hull-House Association Board of Trustees Papers, Special Collections, University of Illinois at Chicago.

51. Florence Scala to Norman Parker, April 9, 1961, University Archives, University of Illinois at Chicago.

52. One suburban leader, trying to attract the university to his region, wrote, "On whose hands will be the blood and agony for the crimes to be committed on co-eds, male students, faculty members and their families by the criminals who are on the increase downtown? Most of those who want to give up Garfield Park do so because it is over-run by criminals. Harrison–Halsted is bad now and would be worse if the university went there and upset their churches and business district. I do not think we should antagonize 200,000 Spanish descent people, or any other people." Karl Treen, Vice President Regional Association of South Cook–Will County Municipalities, to Dean C. C. Caveny, University of Illinois, Navy Pier, February 12, 1961, University Archives, University of Illinois at Chicago.

53. Authors such as Rosalyn Deutsche argue that the media must be seen as a continuum of public space from the perspective of democratic debate. Rosalyn Deutsche, *Evictions: Art and Spatial Politics* (Cambridge: MIT Press, 1996).

54. Iris Marion Young, "Impartiality and the Civic Public," *Throwing Like a Girl and Other Essays in Feminist Philosophy and Social Theory* (Bloomington: Indiana University Press, 1990), 97.

55. "U. of I. Site Hassle in Mayor's Office," *Chicago's American*, April 19, 1961.

56. "Summary of the Meeting at the Offices of Skidmore Owens and Merrill, April 6, 1961," University Archives, University of Illinois at Chicago.

57. Jack Mabley, "U of I—Off Pier into the Slums," *Chicago Daily News*, February 11, 1961; Mabley, "It Will Be a Beautiful Campus but—," *Chicago's American*, September 15, 1961.

58. Jack Mabley, "U. of I. Site D-Day: Honor or Progress, *Chicago's American*, April 25, 1961.

59. Editorial, "Mabley's University Stand," *Chicago's American*, April 26, 1961.

60. John Madigan, on *Standpoint*, WBBM-TV Chicago, broadcast March 22, 1962.

61. John Madigan, on *Standpoint*, WBBM-TV Chicago, broadcast April 23, 1962.

62. John Madigan, on *Standpoint*, WBBM-TV Chicago, broadcast October 19, 1962.

63. Scala, interview by Remini and Beuttler, July 30, 1998.

64. "U. of I. Site Hassle in Mayor's Office," *Chicago's American*, April 19, 1961; "U. of I. Site Row in Daley's Office," *Chicago Sun-Times*, October 10, 1962; "You Can't Stop U. of I., Daley to Site Pickets," *Chicago's American*, October 15, 1962.

65. *Harrison–Halsted Community Group, Inc., et al. v. Housing and Home Finance Agency, et al.,* U.S. Court of Appeals for the Seventh Circuit, September Term and Session 1962, docket number 13860, November 28, 1962, 9.

66. M. W. Newman, "A Tragedy Called Progress Stalks UI Site," *Chicago Daily News*, April 6, 1963.

67. "Highest Court Upholds U.I. Campus Site," *Chicago Tribune*, May 14, 1963. The image accompanying this article is of three women, Jessie Binford (the last resident at Hull-House), Lee Valentino, and Florence Scala meeting with reporters at Hull-House.

68. William F. Deknatel, president, Hull-House Association, to Friends of Hull House, May 1961; testimony presented on behalf of the Hull House Board of Trustees

before the Housing and Planning Committee of the Chicago City Council on Monday, April 17, 1961; all in Hull-House Association Board of Trustees Papers, Special Collections, University of Illinois at Chicago.

69. Hull House, May 3, 1961, Norman A. Parker Papers, University Archives, University of Illinois at Chicago.

70. Press release from the office of Senator Paul H. Douglas (D.-Ill.) July 10, 1961, a.m., Hull-House Association Board of Trustees Papers, Special Collections, University of Illinois at Chicago. It should not be surprising that at a meeting with the campus planners on July 12, 1961, Mayor Daley "was particularly interested in the location of Hull-House and asked Parker what uses would be made of it." "Memorandum of Meeting Held in SOM," July 12, 1961, University Archives, University of Illinois at Chicago.

71. In a letter dated September 6, 1961, to H. Daniel Carpenter, director of the Hudson Guild in New York, Parker suggested a "combination of uses as a Headquarters for the National Training Center [for settlement and neighborhood center workers] and a Jane Addams museum of Social Welfare." He included a confidential rough draft of a memorandum, dated September 3, 1961, recommending this joint program in cooperation with the Jane Addams Graduate School of Social Work. Hull-House Association Board of Trustees Papers, Special Collections, University of Illinois at Chicago.

72. Austin C. Wehrwein, "Campaign to Save Hull House Begun," *New York Times,* July 12, 1963.

73. Georgie Anne Geyer, "Hull House Restoration Pace Picks Up," *Chicago Daily News,* August 10, 1963. Analysis of historic photographs also demonstrates that there was a great deal of inaccuracy in the restoration of the buildings as well; the exterior of the house was modeled on an image of the original building now believed to have been painted in 1896. By the time of this painting, the original building had already been greatly altered.

74. Leonard J. Currie, dean, "Some Notes on the Restoration of Hull House," to Mr. Harry J. Scharres, commissioner, Commission on Chicago Architectural Landmarks, August 7, 1963, Art Institute of Chicago, P-25793.

5. *"Model of the Modern Urban University"*

1. Paul Venable Turner, *Campus,* 140.

2. Parker, "Mission Statement."

3. John Morris Dixon, "Campus City Chicago," *Architectural Forum* 122 (September 1965): 24.

4. See Austin C. Wehrwein, "Illinois U. Unit All Set to Move," *New York Times,* February 14, 1965; "University Opens in Chicago," *New York Times,* February 23, 1965; "By the Cloverleaf," *Time,* January 7, 1966, 57–59; Andrew Schiller, "Chicago's Oxford on the Rocks: A New Break for City Youngsters," *Harpers,* May 1965, 87–94; and "The New Environment: Building Campuses from the Ground Up," *Fortune,* November 1964, 160–165.

5. Ira Bach, quoted in Thomas Buck, "Burnham Idea Adopted—54 Years Later," *Chicago Tribune,* June 10, 1962.

6. Chicago Department of City Planning, *Development Plan for the Central Area of Chicago,* 1.

7. Thomas Buck, "U. of I. Campus Seen as Model of Urban College," *Chicago Tribune,* February 15, 1965.

8. Thomas Buck, "Burnham's Dream Realized in U. of I. Chicago Campus," *Commerce Magazine,* May 1962, 15.

9. Ibid., 98.

10. "The University of Illinois Serves Chicago . . . Serves the State," special supplement, *Chicago Daily News,* September 25, 1965, 24. The supplement was paid for by "the advertisers herein to honor the University of Illinois." Some of the articles are reprints or expansions of other articles written in the early 1960s. However, others are one step short of advertising. Thanks to Douglas Garofalo for providing me with this artifact.

11. Ibid., 20, 21.

12. Arlene Norsym, dean, vice president, and associate chancellor for UIC Alumni Relations, interview, March 20, 2008, for *A Tribute to Walter Netsch: Campus Designer and Architect for the University of Illinois at Chicago,* video (Chicago: College of Architecture and the Arts, UIC, 2008).

13. "The University of Illinois Serves Chicago . . . Serves the State," 9.

14. Nathaniel Owings, quoted in Bernard Michael Boyle, "Architectural Practice in America, 1865–1965—Ideal and Reality," in *The Architect: Chapters in the History of the Profession,* ed. Spiro Kostof (New York: Oxford University Press, 1977), 326.

15. Robert Bruegmann, ed., *Modernism at Mid-Century: The Architecture of the United States Air Force Academy* (Chicago: University of Chicago Press, 1994).

16. Walter Netsch, interview by Betty J. Blum, *Oral History of Walter Netsch* (Chicago: Art Institute of Chicago, 1997–2000), 25.

17. Sert's influence came through his book, *Can Our Cities Survive? An ABC of Urban Problems, Their Analysis, Their Solutions; Based on the Proposals Formulated by the C. I. A. M., International Congresses for Modern Architecture* (Cambridge, Mass.: Harvard University Press, 1942). For a provocative history of CIAM and its inroads in the United States, see Eric Mumford, *The CIAM Discourse on Urbanism, 1928–1960* (Cambridge: MIT Press, 2000). Mies van der Rohe in his role as director of the Bauhaus in Germany in the early 1930s was a member but was inactive in the postwar period, working with Ludwig Hilberseimer from their base at IIT in Chicago (ibid., 52, 203–204).

18. In fact, Netsch specifically disavowed a relationship. See Nory Miller, "Evaluation: The University of Illinois' Chicago Campus as Urban Design," *AIA Journal* 66 (January 1977): 26.

19. Mumford, *The CIAM Discourse on Urbanism,* 25, 60.

20. Ibid., 143.

21. Ibid., 181–182.

22. Robert Bruegmann, "Military Culture, Architectural Culture, Popular Culture,"

in Bruegmann, *Modernism at Mid-Century,* 79–101. Note that Bunshaft was a design partner at SOM.

23. Netsch, interview by Beuttler and Remini.

24. See Office of the UIC Historian, "History of the University of Illinois at Chicago," www.uic.edu/depts/uichistory/index.html#timeline (last accessed January 4, 2007), for a timeline of the history of the campus.

25. Subcommittee on Physical Planning for the Chicago Undergraduate Division, "Report on Low, Medium, and High Rise Buildings."

26. Netsch, interview by Beuttler and Remini.

27. The university commissioned numerous internal and external studies. One study anticipated a 141 percent increase in higher education enrollment in Illinois from 1950 to 1977. Technical Research Committee, UIC Senate, *Graphic and Statistical Profile* (Chicago Undergraduate Division, University of Illinois, September 1958), University Archives, University of Illinois at Chicago.

28. "Criteria for Evaluation of Harrison–Halsted Site," December 7, 1960, University Archives, University of Illinois at Chicago.

29. "Memorandum of Meeting Held in SOM," July 12, 1961, University Archives, University of Illinois at Chicago.

30. A full display of the model was shown in the November 1960 bulletin of the West Central Association, a business group organized around the redevelopment of the West Side; bulletin in the University Archives, University of Illinois at Chicago.

31. Charles Havens to Chancellor Parker, "Rough Draft: May 19, 1971, Outline of Material on Site Selection Following Meeting with 'Mr. Rotstein' on May 6, 1971," University Archives, University of Illinois at Chicago.

32. See RERC, *"Analysis of Sites,"* reports dated 1954, [1955?], and October 1958, University Archives, University of Illinois at Chicago.

33. Netsch, interview by Beuttler and Remini. Reproductions of undated sketches at SOM Chicago suggest that there were four schematic plans, of which three are extant: "grouped by curricula," "grouped by building type," and "grouped by college and enrollment."

34. University Building Program Committee, "A Ten-Year Building Space Estimate for Development of a General Campus Plan" conveyed to Gordon N. Ray, vice president and provost, August 14, 1959, internally distributed February 8, 1960, University Archives, University of Illinois at Chicago. Of all of the principles, the failure to provide adequate provisions for handicapped access proved to be among the most problematic as expansion of the university continued.

35. "Report of the Interim Committee to Advise Concerning Physical Planning for the Chicago Undergraduate Division Campus," December 1960, 3, University Archives, University of Illinois at Chicago. This report documented twenty-seven meetings among the committee, representatives of the university, and representatives of the architect.

36. Ibid., 1–2.

37. Ibid., 8.

38. Ibid.

39. Netsch, interview by Beuttler and Remini.

40. Ibid.

41. These are Iris Marion Young's terms. Young, "Impartiality and the Civic Public," 95.

42. Dixon, "Campus City Chicago."

43. Sasaki, Dawson, and Associates (subsequently Sasaki, Dawson, and DeMay) appear to have received the commission because they were already working for the University of Illinois on projects for the Urbana–Champaign campus. Dan Kiley was the landscape architect for Netsch's Air Force Academy designs, where his use of flat surfaces and modular grids reinforced the axial planning and strict geometries of the campus. Dawson's work on the project dates from the summer of 1961 and has never been published. The landscape plans that were published and from which the campus was built are SOM's. See, for example, *Inland Architect* 9 (November 1965): 12–17.

44. What remains unclear is the extent to which these diagrams directly influenced the final design. The sketches remaining in SOM's archive appear to have been developed for the September presentation, but most features of the design were in place by May.

45. EFL, *Bricks and Mortarboards,* preface.

46. The UICC campus was one of three case studies discussed at the first annual conference of the Society for College and University Planning, Portland State College, August 13–14, 1966. Frederick W. Mayer, ed., *Contrasting Concepts in Campus Planning: Selected Papers from the First Annual Conference* (Ann Arbor, Mich.: Society for College and University Planning, 1967).

47. Mel Elfin, "Classrooms," in EFL, *Bricks and Mortarboards,* 31.

48. Netsch, interview by Beuttler and Remini.

49. James J. Morisseau, "Campus," in EFL, *Bricks and Mortarboards,* 133, 134.

50. Ibid., 150, 152.

51. Ibid., 151.

52. Press release, April 18, 1962, University Archives, University of Illinois at Chicago.

53. Oscar Newman, "The New Campus," *Architectural Forum* 124 (May 1966): 45.

54. Boyer, *Dreaming the Rational City,* 272, 276.

55. Ibid., 270.

56. "Everyman's University," *Chicago Daily News,* September 16, 1961.

57. Thomas Buck, "Chicago Circle—A National Model," in "The University of Illinois Serves Chicago," 16.

58. Dean Raymond W. Coleman, quoted in Thomas Buck, "Circle Campus—All New Pioneering 'U,'" *Chicago Tribune,* February 16, 1965.

59. Buck, "Circle Campus." The television monitors and slide projectors were replaced by digital projectors and computers beginning in the late 1990s.

60. "P/A Observer, University of Illinois, Chicago Campus: Transition, Tradition, or New Approach?" *Progressive Architecture* 46 (October 1965): 226.

61. Ibid., 231.

62. Among the best known are the campuses at the State University of New York (SUNY) at Albany (Edward Durell Stone, 1961) and the University of California at Irvine (William L. Pereira & Associates, 1963).

63. Newman, "The New Campus," 43–45.

64. Leonard Currie, quoted in "P/A Observer, University of Illinois, Chicago Campus," 226.

6. Campus Revolt

1. See Royko, *Boss,* 11–15.

2. "U. I. Circle Campus Is Lauded," *Chicago Tribune,* October 14, 1965.

3. Clark Kerr, *The Uses of the University* (Cambridge, Mass.: Harvard University Press, 1963), 18–19.

4. Ibid., 87–88. Kerr did not coin the phrase "knowledge industry." It is often ascribed to the management consultant Peter Drucker, but it is not clear whether he was the first to use the phrase either.

5. Ibid., 41.

6. Stanley Aronowitz, *The Knowledge Factory: Dismantling the Corporate University and Creating True Higher Learning* (Boston: Beacon Press, 2000), 33.

7. Mario Savio, address on Sproul Hall Steps, December 2, 1964, http://www.lib.berkeley.edu/MRC/saviotranscript.html (last accessed May 14, 2005). The University of California at Berkeley maintains a large online catalogue of material from this period in its history.

8. George Nash, *The University and the City: Eight Cases of Involvement* (New York: McGraw-Hill, 1973), 1.

9. Jennifer Lawrence, presentation of *Berkeley 2020* at the College of Urban Planning and Public Affairs, University of Illinois at Chicago, April 29, 2005. See "Welcome to the New Century," http://www.cp.berkeley.edu/ncp/index.html for the Berkeley New Century plan (last accessed December 30, 2006).

10. Jacobs and Scala knew of each other's work and appear to have met at some point in the early 1960s. Geyer, "The Heritage of Jane Addams," 22–27; Jacobs, *The Death and Life of Great American Cities.*

11. "Slum Blight: Chicago's Number One Target," *Architectural Forum* 116 (May 1962): 119.

12. Marshall Berman, *All That Is Solid Melts into Air: The Experience of Modernity* (1982; repr., New York: Penguin Books, 1988), 295–296. Berman astutely noted, "*The Death and Life of Great American Cities* gives us the first fully articulated woman's view of the city since Jane Addams" (322).

13. Henri Lefebvre, "The Right to the City," in *Writings on Cities,* trans. and ed. Eleonore Kofman and Elizabeth Lebas (Oxford: Blackwell, 1996), 103; originally published in French (1968). Berman was separated from Lefebvre by an ocean and at least a generation, but their writings on cities are similarly informed by Marxist theory and 1960s revolutions.

14. Henri Lefebvre, *The Production of Space*, trans. Donald Nicholson-Smith (Cambridge, Mass.: Blackwell, 1991), 317; originally published as *La Production de l'espace* (1974).

15. It has been said that Netsch located the chancellor on the twenty-eighth floor and provided a separate elevator to it specifically to prevent occupation by students. I find little evidence to support this claim. The tower was designed well in advance of the student sit-ins of the late 1960s, and Netsch and the university trustees were probably more concerned with the spectacular views of the city than with urban defense.

16. Peter Blake, *Form Follows Fiasco: Why Modern Architecture Doesn't Work* (Boston: Little, Brown, 1977); and Charles A. Jencks, *The Language of Post-Modern Architecture* (New York: Rizzoli, 1977).

17. James Corner, "Eidetic Operations and New Landscapes," in *Recovering Landscape: Essays in Contemporary Landscape Architecture*, ed. James Corner (New York: Princeton Architectural Press, 1999), 155.

18. Boyer, *Dreaming the Rational City*, 274.

19. Dixon, "Campus City Chicago," 23–44.

20. M. W. Newman, "Academe in Metropolis: A Critical Appraisal of Chicago Circle," *Chicago Daily News Panorama*, October 2, 1965.

21. Ibid.

22. Christopher Jencks and David Riesman, *The Academic Revolution* (New York: Doubleday, 1968), 182. It is worth noting that Jencks's and Riesman's writings have been critiqued for their racial, gender, and class biases. However, their sentiments regarding the problems of commuter campuses were echoed by other authors at the time.

23. Alan Colquhoun, "Postmodernism and Structuralism: A Retrospective Glance," *Assemblage* 5 (February 1988): 8.

24. Anthony Vidler, Editorial, *Oppositions* 17 (Summer 1979): 3.

25. Miller, "Evaluation," 26–27.

26. Ibid., 31.

27. Ibid. During the economic problems of the mid-1970s, university officials also began to cut back on regular maintenance, leading to problems that still exist today.

28. I am not suggesting that Tigerman or his colleagues were responsible for these changes, only that his comments reflected the sentiments of many at the university.

29. Justin O'Brien and Laurent Pernot, quoted in "The Last Goodbye," *UIC News*, April 28, 1993.

30. Robert Bruegmann, "Build Up, Don't Tear Down, Campus Landmarks," *UIC News*, September 16, 1962.

31. Blair Kamin, "The Transformation of UIC: Design Puts Humanity Back in the Equation," *Chicago Tribune*, October 29, 1995.

32. Cheryl Kent, "Softening Brutalism: Is Anything Lost?" *Architectural Record* 184 (August 1996): 22.

33. The university is once again undergoing a master planning process by the architecture firm Booth Hansen and the landscape architecture firm Hargreaves Associates.

34. See, for example, Roger Flaherty, "UIC Gains Clout in Research, but Some See Shortchanging of Undergrads," *Chicago Sun-Times,* June 26, 1990; and Greg Beaubien, "Buffing Up UIC," *Chicago Tribune,* January 11, 1995.

7. City as Campus

1. Perry and Wiewel, *The University as Urban Developer.*

2. Initiative for a Competitive Inner City (ICIC) and CEOs for Cities, *Leveraging Colleges and Universities for Urban Revitalization: An Action Agenda* (Boston: CEOs for Cities, [2002?]), 6, 19; www.icic.org/site/c.fnJNKPNhFiG/b.3908857/k.7600/ Publications_Archive.htm (last accessed August 2010).

3. Robert Campbell, "Universities Are the New City Planners," *Boston Globe,* March 20, 2005. Campbell was summarizing the discussions of a panel that he moderated for the American Academy of Arts and Sciences on January 28, 2005. Participants included Lee Bollinger, president of Columbia University; Omar Blaik, senior vice president of the University of Pennsylvania; James Polshek of Polshek Partnership Architects LLP; and E. John Rosenwald Jr. of Bear Stearns Companies.

4. ICIC and CEOs for Cities, *Leveraging Colleges and Universities for Urban Revitalization,* 7. The authors of this document also note that fully half of the institutions of higher education are located in the "urban core."

5. See, for example, Charles Madigan, ed., *Global Chicago* (Chicago: University of Illinois Press, 2004); and Janet L. Abu-Lughod, *New York, Chicago, Los Angeles: America's Global Cities* (Minneapolis: University of Minnesota Press, 1999).

6. Arjun Appadurai, "Grassroots Globalization and the Research Imagination," in *Globalization,* ed. Arjun Appadurai (Durham, N.C.: Duke University Press, 2001), 1–21.

7. As of this writing, there are seventeen campuses covered in this series, including the University of Chicago and the Illinois Institute of Technology.

8. Alice Sinkevitch, *AIA Guide to Chicago,* 2nd ed. (San Diego, Calif.: Harvest Books, 2004).

9. See, for example, Bluestone, "Preservation and Renewal in Post–World War II Chicago," 210–223.

10. The other competitors were Zaha Hadid, Peter Eisenman, Kazuyo Sejima, and Helmut Jahn. See, for example, Lee Bey, "IIT Panel Chooses Architect," *Chicago Sun-Times,* February 2, 1998; Blair Kamin, "IIT's New Groove Tube: Its Campus Is Rated among the Ugliest, but the School That Mies Built Is Fighting Back—with What Else, Splashy Architecture," *Chicago Tribune,* May 16, 2002; Christopher Hawthorne, "ABC's of Mies + IIT: Koolhaas's New Student Center Is Both a Tribute to the Master and a Challenge," *Metropolis* 23 (February 2004): 676–681; and Suzanne Stephens, "Iconoclasm Invades Iconic Territory with Rem Koolhaas's Design for the New IIT Campus Center in Chicago," *Architectural Record* 192 (May 2004): 122–129.

11. Rem Koolhaas, "Miestakes," in Lambert, *Mies in America,* 724.

12. "IIT beyond Mies: A New Urban Focus," *Praxis* 1 (1999): 15.

13. Leroy E. Kennedy, presentation at the College of Urban Planning and Public Affairs, UIC, April 29, 2005. The demolition of almost all of Chicago's high-rise public housing and the redevelopment of these sites as part of the CHA's *Plan for Transformation* is highly contested and beyond the scope of this book.

14. See Peter Lindsey Schaudt, "Rehabilitation in Context: Alfred Caldwell's Planting Design for the Illinois Institute of Technology—Rediscovered and Interpreted," *Vineyard: An Occasional Record of the National Park Service Historic Landscape Initiative* 2 (2000): 11–13.

15. The university's master plan uses the term "gothic," but a more commonplace architectural reference would be "neo-Gothic" to indicate the use and principles of Gothic architecture within the context of a modern revival dating to the late nineteenth century.

16. Wim Wiewel, "Colleges as Catalysts: Rebuilding Urban Communities," presentation to the AIA 2004 National Convention, Chicago, June 12, 2004.

17. Robert Becker, "Woodlawn Watches Warily as U. of C. Stretches South," *Chicago Tribune,* October 12, 2004.

18. "South Campus Planning," "Letter to Woodlawn Neighbors," October 15, 2004, http://southcampusplan.uchicago.edu/letter.html (last accessed August 18, 2010).

19. NBBJ, *The University of Chicago Campus Master Plan,* 79.

20. Ibid., 6.

21. Ibid., 26.

22. For community responses to university development, particularly within its South Campus, see, for example, Jeremy Adragna, "Herald Coverage," September 15, 2004, http://www.hydepark.org/hpkccnews/socampusplan.htm#coverage (last accessed June 6, 2005).

23. Rosen, *Decision-Making Chicago Style.*

24. "Tax Increment Financing (TIF) is a technique that local governments use for financing (re)development activities. A local government designates an area for improvement, demonstrating that the area meets the eligibility requirements set out in the state's enabling legislation, and drafts a redevelopment plan of improvements it expects to see take place within the designated boundaries of the TIF district. The local government often subsidizes developers to make these improvements. As property values in the area rise and taxes increase, the local government uses the future growth in property tax revenues to pay off the initial and ongoing economic development expenditures." Rachel Webber and Laura Goddeeris, "Tax Increment Financing: Process and Planning Issues," prepared for Lincoln Institute of Land Policy Fiscal Dimensions of Planning Program (2006), 2.

25. See, for example, Webber, Theodore, and Hoch, "Private Choices and Public Obligations."

26. These developers and architects included, among others, Mesirow Stein Real

Estate as the master developers, Wight & Company as the master planners, and Bauer Latoza Studio for new and rehabilitated buildings along Halsted Street.

27. Courtney Challos, "Maxwell St. Buildings, Preservation Hopes Come Tumbling Down," *Chicago Tribune*, August 13, 2000.

28. Lee Bey, "Assessing History at Face Value," *Chicago Sun-Times*, September 2, 1999.

29. Blair Kamin, "Mockery on Maxwell Street: City Loses Market Value with Paste-On Project Proposal," *Chicago Tribune*, October 15, 1999.

30. Frances Halsband, "Campuses in Place," *Places* 17 (Spring 2005): 8, 11.

31. Skidmore, Owings & Merrill (SOM), principal consultants, *The Chicago Central Area Plan: Preparing the Central City for the 21st Century*, recommendations to the Central Area Plan Steering Committee (Chicago, July 2002), 2.10.

32. Greater State Street Council and the Central Michigan Avenue Association, "Executive Summary," in *Higher Education in the Loop and South Loop: An Impact Study* (Chicago: January 2005).

33. SOM, *The Chicago Central Area Plan*, 3.12.

34. Ibid., 3.71.

35. McGuire Igleski & Associates, Inc., *Columbia College Chicago Campus Preservation Plan*, vol. 1 ([Chicago?], June 2005), also at www.lib.colum.edu/archhistory/about.htm (last accessed August 2010).

36. Gary Washburn, "Dorm Set for South Loop Site: 3 Colleges to Build 18-Story Facility on Bargain Land," *Chicago Tribune*, September 25, 2001.

37. Amber Holst, quoted in John Handley, "In Residence: Construction of Downtown Dorms Is Bringing More Students into the Loop," *Chicago Tribune*, September 10, 2000; see also Jodi S. Cohen, "Great Student Mixer: Four Colleges + One Dorm = Housing Model," *Chicago Tribune*, November 6, 2005.

38. Tony Jones, quoted in William Mullen, "Chicago Art Institute Converts Historic Loop Office Buildings to Dorm," *Chicago Tribune*, September 4, 1997.

39. Handley, "In Residence."

40. For financial reasons connected to its parent institution, the Art Institute of Chicago, the school has since sold a number of the buildings it had purchased. The increase in students desiring to live near their downtown campuses has also sparked new privately built off-campus housing near both the Loop universities and UIC. See Alby Gallun, "Not Your Daddy's Dorm," *Crain's Chicago Business*, July 25, 2005.

41. Valerio Dewalt Train Associates and Goody Clancy and Associates, *Columbia College Chicago Masterplan* ([Chicago?], March 2006), also at www2.colum.edu/masterplan/pdfdownloads.html (last accessed August 2010).

42. Lee Bey, "Loop Dorm Repeats the Past," *Chicago Sun-Times*, August 28, 2000.

43. Blair Kamin, "Dorm Trying Too Hard to Fit Neighborhood: University Center at State and Congress Is Saddled with Old Ideas," *Chicago Tribune*, September 19, 2004.

44. Blair Kamin, "Roosevelt University Building a Glass Tower of Its Own," *Chicago*

Tribune, August 9, 2010, featuresblogs.chicagotribune.com/theskyline/2010/08/
roosevelt-university-building-a-glass-tower-of-its-own.html (last accessed August
2010).

45. Alicia Berg, quoted in John Handley, "Three Chicago Universities Collaborate
to Build Dormitory Downtown," *Chicago Tribune*, January 20, 2002.

46. Appadurai, "Grassroots Globalization and the Research Imagination," 5;
See also Manuel Castells, *The Informational City: Information, Technology, Economic
Restructuring, and the Urban-Regional Process* (Cambridge, Mass.: Blackwell, 1989);
David Harvey, *The Condition of Postmodernity: An Enquiry into the Origins of Cultural
Change* (Cambridge, Mass.: Blackwell, 1989); and Edward W. Soja, *Postmodern Ge-
ographies: The Reassertion of Space in Critical Social Theory* (New York: Verso, 1989).

47. Saskia Sassen, *Cities in a World Economy* (London: Pine Forge Press, 1994), 4.

Conclusion

1. Marilyn Taylor, "Crossing beyond the Boundaries: Columbia University in
West Harlem," *Places* 17 (Spring 2005): 51. It is worth noting that as of this writing, Taylor has been named the dean of the University of Pennsylvania's School
of Design. Penn has recently purchased twenty-four acres of land adjacent to the
Schuylkill River that it intends to develop as "a mix of residential, commercial and
academic buildings anchored by promenades and lawns with an unobstructed view
of center city." Angela Couloumbus, "Penn Sees Postal Site as Gateway," *Philadelphia
Inquirer*, January 20, 2004.

2. Ira Harkavy, quoted in Martin van der Werf, "Urban Universities Try New
Ways to Reach Out to Their Communities," *Chronicle of Higher Education* 45 (April
30, 1999): A37.

3. Ira Harkavy and John L. Pucket, "Lessons from Hull House for the Contemporary Urban University," *Social Service Review* 68 (September 1, 1994): 300.

4. Ibid., 301.

5. Press release, "New Jersey Offers Cash Incentive to Boost Home Owner-
ship Near Urban Colleges and Universities," January 6, 2000, www.state.nj.us/dca/
news/2000/pro10600.htm (last accessed June 16, 2005); Rachelle Garbarine, "Fostering the Links of Colleges to Neighborhoods," *New York Times*, October 16, 2002.
The program was later enlarged to include additional schools and neighborhoods.

6. James R. Hardcastle, "Howard University Looks to Its Neighborhood," *New
York Times*, April 4, 1999; Rudolph A. Pyatt Jr., "In LeDroit Park, Howard Is Teaching
by Example," *Washington Post*, December 28, 1998.

7. V. Dion Haynes, "Howard to Put Innovations to the Test," *Washington Post*,
March 6, 2005.

8. Stephen Sterrett, "The University on Main Street: Commercial Revitalization
in the Campus Community," poster presentation, Outreach Scholarship 2004 Conference, State College, Pennsylvania, October 3–5, 2004; Campus Partners, "University Neighborhood Revitalization Plan Concept Document" (July 1996), www.
campuspartners.osu.edu/plan.htm (last accessed June 2005). Also Laura Shinn,

of the Office of Facilities Planning and Development at the Ohio State University, and Stephen A. Sterrett, of Campus Partners for Community Urban Redevelopment, interview with author, April 22, 2005; Laura Shinn, "Colleges as Catalysts," presentation at the AIA National Convention, Chicago, June 10, 2004; and David Dixon, "Campus Partners and the Ohio State University: Transforming a Failing Commercial District," *Places* 17 (Spring 2005): 47. In the end, this may prevent the university from being seen as an agent of displacement and gentrification.

9. Garbarine, "Fostering the Links of Colleges to Neighborhoods." University of Pennsylvania is not the only Ivy League, research university to work in close collaboration with its city and neighborhoods. The joint study by ICIC and CEOs for Cities, *Leveraging Colleges and Universities for Urban Economic Revitalization*, highlights a number of universities and their initiatives, including large programs at Yale and Columbia universities.

10. *West Philadelphia Initiatives: A Case Study in Urban Revitalization* (Philadelphia: University of Pennsylvania, undated [2004?]), 8, www.fels.upenn.edu/news/ new-report-urban-revitalization-1 (last accessed June 22, 2005). As in the case of Columbia University, students at Penn demonstrated against expansion in the 1960s. Here the target of protest was the expansion of the science center in early 1969 that was reported by the *New York Times* as part of a wave of campus protests over a variety of issues involving campus life, curricula, and military recruitment at that time. See "Students at Roosevelt U. [Chicago] Seize Office of the President in Protest," *New York Times*, February 21, 1969. See also Elizabeth Strom, "The Political Strategies behind University-Based Development: Two Philadelphia Cases," in Perry and Wiewel, *The University as Urban Developer*, Perry and Wiewel, 116–130.

11. *West Philadelphia Initiatives*, 9.

12. Ibid., 19.

13. Lee Bollinger, quoted in Nancy Levinson, "Campus Planning Is Breaking New Ground," *Architectural Record* 192 (August 2004): 92.

14. Taylor, "Crossing beyond the Boundaries," 51.

15. Designed by Marilyn Jordan Taylor of Skidmore, Owings & Merrill and the Renzo Piano Building Workshop.

16. David Dinkins, "Don't Fear Columbia," *New York Times*, May 27, 2007; see also Jimmy Vielkind, "In the Community, Some Expansion Doubts, *Columbia Spectator*, April 23, 2004.

17. Embraced by city officials, the new campus is scorned by some faculty, many of whom either do not want to move across the river or question the way in which the university is expanding its academic mission. Although the university has been acquiring land in Allston for decades—until 1997 unknown to the public—the project became aligned with former Harvard president Larry Summers. Through a number of public statements, new curricular proposals, and decisions regarding faculty control, Summers angered the core faculty in the Liberal Arts and Sciences, who equated Allston development with the "corporatization of Harvard." Michael Ryan, "Painting the Town Crimson," *Boston Globe*, October 24, 2004. See also James Atlas, "The Battle behind the Battle at Harvard," *New York Times*, February 27, 2005; and

Rachel Donadio, "The Tempest in the Ivory Tower," *New York Times Book Review*, March 27, 2005: 12–13.

18. Harvard University, "2007 Harvard University Allston Campus Institutional Master Plan Notification Form," January 11, 2007, 1, 5.

19. The master plan is under the guidance of the Allston Development Group and urban planning teams at Cooper, Robertson & Partners and landscape architect Laurie Olin, with input from the architect Frank Gehry.

20. Harvard University reports on the Allston Initiative via the Web at http://www.allston.harvard.edu/ (last accessed January 1, 2007).

21. Frank Gehry has been involved in the master plan process in what appears to be a sketch of the possible forms of the new civic buildings. Behnisch Architects of Stuttgart, Germany, have designed the new 4.7 acre Science Complex, and the young firm of Daly Genick Architects from Los Angeles has been engaged to renovate buildings for the Harvard University Art Museum.

22. At the time of this writing, there is concern that the designs for individual components of the campus are moving ahead in advance of a master plan for the entire area. See the editorial "Colleges as City Builders," *Boston Globe,* November 16, 2006. In light of current economic realities, the university is also delaying construction on its own projects.

23. Charles V. Bagli, "Court Upholds Columbia Campus Expansion Plan," *New York Times,* June 23, 2010.

24. Robin Pogrebin, "N.Y.U. Plans to Expand Its Campuses by 40 Percent," *New York Times,* March 23, 2010. The article noted that the interview with President Sexton was conducted via telephone, as he was in Qatar, where the university is building a campus in Abu Dhabi. A summary of and arguments for the plan can be found at http://www.nyu.edu/nyu2031/nyuinnyc/ (last accessed August 2010).

25. Mark C. Taylor, "Academic Bankruptcy," *New York Times,* August 14, 2010. See also Taylor, "Controlling the Crisis on Campus," *Forbes.com,* August 11, 2010, www.forbes.com/2010/08/01/crisis-college-campus-education-opinions-best-colleges-10-taylor.html (last accessed August 2010); and Taylor, *Crisis on Campus: A Bold Plan for Reforming Our Colleges and Universities* (New York: Knopf, forthcoming). Note that the description of Taylor's arguments offered here come from the published articles, not the book, which at the time of this writing has not been released. Among the reforms Taylor recommends in his op-ed pieces, the only recommendation that applies to expansion is a proposal to combine the Philosophy Departments of NYU and Columbia. It would appear that Taylor does not confront many contemporary requirements that are sparking new campus development in areas beyond the core of liberal arts education: clinical and translational sciences, engineering, business schools, professional programs, the arts, and new interdisciplinary institutes and centers. It remains to be seen whether Taylor's concerns apply more to humanities programs *within* today's universities than to the universities as a whole, which often see expansion as a necessary component of global competition and growth into new markets.

26. Readings, *The University in Ruins,* 13.

27. Ibid., 5.

28. Ibid., 169.

29. Sigmund Freud, *Civilization and Its Discontents*, trans. and ed., James Strachey (New York: W. W. Norton, 1961), 17; originally published as *Das Unbehagen in der Kultur* (1930).

30. See Thomas Bender, *Community and Social Change in America* (New Brunswick, N.J.: Rutgers University Press, 1978).

31. Thomas Bender, "Locality and Worldliness," American Council of Learned Societies Occasional Paper no. 40 (1997), http://archives.acls.org/op/op40ben.htm (last accessed August 18, 2005). It is interesting to note that NYU does not have a campus in the traditional sense, although it uses Washington Square Park, which it nominally surrounds, as the image of its campus. See, for example, the university's home page, http://www.nyu.edu/ (last accessed May 16, 2005).

32. Bender, "Scholarship, Local Life, and the Necessity of Worldliness," 21.

33. Bender, "Locality and Worldliness."

34. Arjun Appadurai, *Modernity at Large: Cultural Dimensions of Globalization* (Minneapolis: University of Minnesota Press, 1996), 33. See also "I & I Interviews Arjun Appadurai," *Items and Issues Quarterly* 4 (Winter 2003–2004): 24–27.

35. Appadurai, *Modernity at Large*, 183–184.

36. Janet L. Abu-Lughod, ed., *From Urban Village to East Village: The Battle for New York's Lower East Side* (Cambridge, Mass.: Blackwell, 1994), 5.

37. Mark C. Taylor, "End the University as We Know It," *New York Times*, April 27, 2009.

38. Readings, *The University in Ruins*, 180–193.

39. Iris Marion Young, "City Life and Difference," reprinted in *Metropolis: Center and Symbol of Our Times*, ed. Philip Kasinitz (New York: New York University Press, 1995), 256.

40. Ibid., 264.

41. Ibid., 266.

Index

Turner, Paul Venable, xvi, 26, 203n10
Turrell, James, 166
Twenty Years at Hull-House (Addams), 12, 104

UIC. *See* University of Illinois at Chicago
UICC. *See* University of Illinois at Chicago Circle
UIUC. *See* University of Illinois at Urbana-Champaign
U.S. Air Force Academy, 105, 106, 107, 109, 126, 144, 222n43
U.S. Census Bureau: definition of "urban," 204n9
U.S. Court of Appeals for the Seventh Circuit, 90
U.S. Department of Labor, 35, 36
university: Enlightenment concept of, 197; environment of, xxii; as ruined institution, 201; space for, xiii–xiv
University Center, 175, 176, 177, 179, 182
University of Berlin, 39
University of California at Berkeley, 135, 223n7
University of California at Irvine, 223n62
University of Chicago, xxvii, xxix, 6, 25, 58, 60, 65, 153, 154; Booth School of Business, 161, 162; campus of, 23, 26, 130–31, 160–65; Charles M. Harper Center, 161, 162; formulation of, 7; Gerald Ratner Athletics Center, 161; growth of, xxvii, 27, 160–65; Hull-House and, xxviii, 29–30, 38, 42–43; Hyde Park and, 63, 67, 133; Kenwood and, 63, 67, 133; Laird Bell Law Quadrangle, 63, 164; master plan for, 23, 24, 161, 162; Max Pavelsky Residential Commons, 161; North Campus of, 63, 164; organization of, 47; Regenstein Library, 161; Reva and David Logan Center for Creative Performing Arts, 161;

scale comparison of, 156; School of Social Service Administration, 42, 43; settlement organized by, 10–11; South Campus of, 63, 162–63, 164, 226n22; urban renewal and, 53, 61–62, 66, 68; Woodward Court Women's Dormitory, 63
University of Illinois, 67, 69, 71, 75, 77, 85, 213n1, 214n6, 220n10, 222n43; baby-boom students and, 55; expansion of, 72; map of, 3; new campus and, 58
University of Illinois at Chicago (UIC), xxvii, 8, 71, 144, 145, 146, 147, 148, 153, 154, 171, 173, 227n40; buildings at, 179–80; Chicago Circle interchange and, 143; dormitories at, 145; East Campus, 147, 168; entrance to, 7; expansion of, 165; Hull-House and, 29–30, 38, 42–43; neighborhood and, 168; proposal for, 55; rendering of, 56; scale comparison of, 156; South Campus of, 165–66, 167, 168, 169, 170, 180, 183, 190; transformation of, 146; University Village, 165, 166, 170
University of Illinois at Chicago Circle (UICC), 53, 54, 57, 68, 69, 70, 92, 97, 99, 101, 108, 111, 122, 125, 127, 136, 147, 183; accessibility to, 77; aerial view of, 123; building, 81; campus of, 73, 123, 133, 139, 140–41, 143; conceptual organization of, 121; Congress–Halsted site, 100; design for, xxix, 104–7, 113, 120–21; film on, 204n19; Forum, 117, 120, 121, 122, 123, 124, 126, 130, 131, 133, 138, 139, 140, 143, 144, 145, 147, 166, 200; Harrison–Halsted site, 115; Hull-House and, 81, 94, 95, 110; landscape plan for, 116, 119; Lecture Center, 114, 116, 117, 118, 120, 121, 122, 127; location of, 70–81, 86, 175; mission of, 98, 104; opening of, 126; plan for, 117, 118; protesting,

88, 89; scheme for, 115; Sears and, 102, 103; site for, 78, 90, 92; sketches of, 129; SOM and, xxix, 77, 109, 110, 114, 115, 117, 118; University Hall, 116, 120, 126, 141, 143; upper walkways, 120, 128, 130, 139, 146; urban character of, 77, 106, 129

University of Illinois at Urbana–Champaign (UIUC), 3, 70–71, 72, 73, 108

University of Illinois board of trustees, 107–8

University of Illinois Foundation, 93–94

University of Illinois Medical Center, 143, 147, 162

"University of Illinois Serves Chicago . . . Serves the State, The" (supplement), 102, 103

University of Mexico campus, 106–7

University of Pennsylvania, 66, 186, 229n10; Cartographic Modeling Laboratory, 188; Center for Community Partnerships, 186; investment/development decisions and, 188; neighborhood revitalization projects and, 187–88; University City Science Center, 188

University of Virginia, xxiv, 58–59; as academical village, xxii; campus of, xxiii–xxiv; design of, xxiv

urban campus, xiv, xvii, xxiv–xxv, 74, 149; concept of, 57–58; globalization and, 196–201; opposing spaces and, xxii; precedents for design of, 104–7; urban renewal and, 66

urban design, 29, 59, 60–61, 105, 108, 141, 175, 193, 197, 211n11, 211n21; goals of, xv; UICC and, 106

urban development, xxvi, 25, 30, 52, 68, 82, 91, 106, 189, 210n1

Urban Disorder and the Shape of Belief (Smith), 6

urban environment, 16, 39–40, 53, 137,

186, 192; design implications and, xiv; UICC and, 129; university development and, 24

urban growth, xxvi, 75, 150, 154; dislocations created by, 137; urban renewal and, 53

urban institutions, xxvi, 51, 60

urbanism, xxvi, xxix, 14, 49, 55, 105–6, 108, 136, 142, 165, 170, 179, 185, 195, 200, 298; architecture and, 58; critiques of, 140; knowledge and, xiv; rejection of, 146, 168; as spatial practice, 138

urbanization, xv, xxviii, 2, 7, 31, 105–6, 133, 183

urban life, 30, 36, 38, 70, 74, 150

urban living: instructions for, 30–33, 35

urban mission, 70, 197; designing for, 107–14, 116, 118

urban planning, xxv, xxvi, xxix, xxx, 33, 68, 118, 136, 137, 138, 140, 150, 193, 211n21

urban renewal, xxvi, xxvii, xxix, xxx, 14, 38, 45, 50, 72, 85–86, 91, 98, 119, 136, 138, 139, 142, 150, 151, 155, 161, 188, 211n10, 212n30; campus and, 58–68, 100; displacements caused by, 52; higher education and, 53, 79; model for, 187; politics of, 53; process of, 70; protesting, xxix, 90, 133, 137; racial dynamics of, 65; reassessing, 136–38; repairing wounds of, 185–89; universities and, 53–57; University of Chicago and, 53, 61–62, 66, 68

Urban Renewal Administration, 51

urban space, xxx, 52, 59, 99, 135, 183, 193; battles over, xxvi; higher education and, xx; realignment of, xxix; transformation of, 54

urban transformation, xiv, xxix, 27, 30, 47, 52, 68, 87, 186, 210n1

urban university, xvi, xxii, 51, 97, 98, 150, 170, 186, 198, 199; expansion of, 68; model of, xxix; public/private,

79; purpose-built, xxviii; transparency/interdependency and, 189
Uses of the University (Kerr), 134

Valentino, Lee, 218n67
Van Vaulkenberg, Michael, 160
Venkatesh, Sudhir, 44, 45, 216n34
Veysey, Laurence E., 209n28
Vidler, Anthony, 142
Viñoly, Rafael, 154
VOA Associates, 161, 175, 181
Von Humboldt, Wilhelm, 39

Wade, Richard, 31
Washington Square Park, 190, 231n31
WBBM-TV Chicago, 89
Webber, Henry S., 61, 212n32
Weese, Ben, 91
White, Lucia, 15
White, Morton, 15
Whiting, Sarah, 59, 60, 211n21

Wight & Company, 227n26
Williamson, K. E., 110
Wirth, Lewis, 43, 68
Wolf Clements and Associates, CPD and, 164
Woodlawn, Illinois, 61, 63, 162, 163, 212n32
World's Columbian Exposition (1893), 23; Court of Honor, 4; Midway Plasiance, 2, 24, 61, 63, 163–64, 183; White City, 2, 4, 33, 153
Wright, Frank Lloyd, 162

Yale University, xviii, 25, 66, 150, 229n9
Yamasaki, Minoru, 139
Ylvisaker, Paul, 51
Young, Iris Marion, 87, 200
Youngren, Ralph, 108–9

zoning, 29, 143, 162

Sharon Haar is associate professor of architecture at the University of Illinois at Chicago. She is the editor of *Schools for Cities: Urban Strategies.*